Pierre Jean-Baptiste Le Grand d'Aussy

The Well-Set Table

in

France

Furniture and Settings for Meals

From the Gauls to the Eighteenth Century

Notes and Translation

by Jim Chevallier

Chez Jim Books

Published by
Chez Jim Books

To contact the editor, e-mail: _jimchev@chezjim.com_

ISBN: 978-1499553185

Table of Contents

About Le Grand d'Aussy's work

The current volume has been extracted, translated and retitled from Pierre Jean-Baptiste Le Grand d'Aussy's classic work on French food and drink, which has come down to us with the slightly misleading title of *Histoire de la vie privée des Français depuis l'origine de la nation jusqu'à nos jours*; that is, "History of the private life of the French from the origin of the nation until our days". Though Le Grand originally intended to produce such a comprehensive work, in practice he only finished the three volumes on food and drink (first published in 1783). Incomplete as these may be in terms of the overall project, they are almost manically thorough in their examination of the specific subject and have remained, over the centuries, some of the prime sources on the subject. Not only do even modern writers continue to draw on them for key information, more than one writer (in both French and English) has shamelessly copied whole stretches of Le Grand's work, well after it was written, and presented it as their own.

Le Grand at one point refers to himself as a "compiler" and certainly one of the strengths of his work is that it brings together a wealth of information drawn from earlier sources, some classics of their respective periods, some profoundly obscure. He began as a Jesuit and brings to his task the methodical, erudite and demanding precision which made the Jesuits so admired as teachers. But his personality – passionate, determined, unsparing, but also compassionate, even witty and sensual – shines through. When he thinks a previous writer has written nonsense, he says so, succinctly. When he feels obliged to work his way through fastidious, if important material, he lets his impatience show. When he includes an anecdote more because it is entertaining than because it is essential, he does so without apology. At the rare moments when he draws on his personal experience or acquaintance, he brings us vividly into the instant.

He is, in a word, not only an informative but a lively and enjoyable writer, but one who, in English, is more often cited than translated at length. The present effort is intended to remedy that, if only in small measure.

About this translation

Le Grand regularly includes sideheads in his text, and most of the headings used here are taken from these. Some have been "promoted" to clarify the work's structure and a few high-level headings have been added to group these conceptually. Exceptionally here, some paragraphs include two sideheads; rather than divide the paragraphs in question; such pairs appear with a slash in the relevant heading. An added heading is indicated by square brackets.

This is not, in any meaningful way, an annotated edition, but certain phrases or references have seemed to require clarification or alternate suggestions; the latter appear here in-line, in square brackets ([]). The alphabetic footnotes are Le Grand's own and originally appeared at the bottom of the physical page in each case.

The titles of the many works cited have been left in French, since presumably those who wish to consult them will be seeking the works in that language.

An overview of Le Grand d'Aussy on furniture and settings for meals

Having reviewed food and drink in the previous chapters, Le Grand begins in the middle of his third volume to explore the furniture, utensils and other objects used to serve these. In the process, he not only itemizes the different objects and materials involved in food service, but provides histories of several of France's more important industries.

He begins with the Gauls, who were variously said to sit on hay or dog skins. The Romans introduced lying on couches, but the Franks preferred sitting upright on stools and benches. Still, hay did not disappear; like grass, it was later strewn about rooms.

A long section on table linen follows this, with a glimpse of the curious habit of "slicing the tablecloth" and a look at the production of linen in France.

Le Grand then reviews lighting from hand-held to artificial, oil-powered candles, before briefly discussing utensils. Curiously, though the fork is generally considered to have come to France in the seventeenth century, one fourteenth century king had a number of them in his treasury.

Drinking vessels evolved from horns and – by some reports – human skulls to more elegant ware. Though Le Grand does not discuss this until later, earthenware would also have been used (as well as wooden goblets, which he does not discuss).

The word *nef* could be translated as "nave", having the same naval connotation, but in fact this ornate table-piece is known by the same name in English. In French, the word *cadenas* – which now refers to a type of lock – also had a similar meaning.

A dresser today is typically in a bedroom, but Le Grand explains how the original term developed from *dresser* – to set up – for a piece of furniture used to set out plate for display; something like what English-speakers know today as a sideboard.

The use of fountains at meals was mainly a medieval custom, though Le Grand cites some later examples as well, before moving to the various materials used to make cooking and serving vessels.

It is in this section that he begins to look as much at French industry as at eating customs. First, he discusses the simplest material for making tableware: earth (or clay). When the French moved to more sophisticated variations on this, they were typically inspired by other cultures. Le Grand tells, at some length, the story of Pallissy's efforts to mimic the Italian faience before briefly telling the famous – and most accepted – tale of how an Italian successfully brought the material to France. Strangely however he then treats this as a myth and tells a very different version, one crediting the innovation to a French town with a similar name. Not only is this an unusual account, the text Le Grand cites does not seem to exist in one common edition of the work he cites. In a word, it seems to be here Le Grand who is in error.

He also more understandably mistakes *madre*, a very rare type of curly-grained wood, for something like porcelain. But the *Trésor de la Langue Française* says that this was a veined wood, taken from the heart and roots of certain trees, used in medieval times to make various tableware.

He is on surer ground in discussing the wide-ranging story of porcelain in France. This started with German efforts to imitate a Chinese product and went through several stages before Madame de Pompadour's support of it became one of her more successful contributions to French culture.

Glass has a surprisingly long history in France. If the Merovingians never matched the Romans in this regard, they nonetheless were skilled for their time. Over the centuries the French often did well in this craft, though more often than not less well than others.

If Le Grand only touches briefly on some more precious materials – jewels, crystal, marble, etc., – it is because these, though used, were relatively rare in French tableware over the centuries. Metals however were more common and he looks at these at some length, starting with the simpler ones: tin, lead and copper. After a brief look at yet another technique from the East – that of varnishing metal sheets – , he begins an extensive exploration of the history of silver in France, starting with the natural riches known under the Gauls. These diminished over the centuries, but the hope of them did fitfully inspire efforts at exploration. Meanwhile, silver work of every sort was made and given in France and Le Grand surveys a dizzying array of various objects made in it before providing a view of one medieval king's collection of objects in both gold and silver, some said to be very ancient even in his time.

This prompts a last glance at two more subjects: enamels and the custom of marking one's arms on objects. Finally Le Grand closes with one of the musings that appear infrequently but memorably through his history:

When one recalls that all these riches had been amassed by a Prince who had inherited a ruined Kingdom, which had had to maintain against England very expensive and very long wars, which finally only enjoyed a very limited revenue, one cannot contain one's surprise.

And ends – writing less than a decade before the Revolution – with these thoughts on his own time:

As Royal power gathered solidity and strength, it stopped making its grandeur known in numerous plate which it displayed in spectacle on certain days. It built magnificent palaces, which all the arts as desired rushed to beautify. There, as in the center of its glory, it has known to concentrate all the Greats, who composed for it a Court as brilliant as it was submissive. Instead of these nefs, these flagons, and these golden platters which it once used to represent it, it surrounded itself with a numerous military and civil Household, which, unfortunately onerous for the State by the excessive multiplication of its members, nonetheless offers to its subjects as to foreigners the united spectacle of magnificence and of strength, of power and of majesty.

But not, we now know, for very much longer.

A brief glossary

A handful of terms which appear here are equally archaic in French and English. While rough approximations might be found in modern English, it has seemed best to leave them in either the original French or archaic English, while providing the following guide to these:

Bougeoir – A candle-holder specifically meant to be carried in the hand.

Chopine – This was a vessel, but above all a measure, roughly equivalent to an English pint, and so to half a French one.

Comfet-box (*drageoir*) – This might simplistically be described as a candy box, except that both the sweets (*dragées* in French) in it and the box itself were typically elegant, even ostentatious.

Crown of the sun (*écu au soleil*) – The French crown coin bore a shield (*écu*), from which it took its name. In one variant, a sun appeared above the shield.

Estamoye – This was a wine vessel with two handles.

Fern-ash-glass (*fougère*) – Fern-ash was long used to make an apparently inferior form of glass (the French text merely uses the word for "fern").

Hanap – This was an ornate goblet, typically presented on ceremonial occasions.

Hyder (*idre*) – A vessel for holding water.

Juste – This is said to have resembled a pitcher, but of a specific size. (*Juste*, meaning "right" or "exact", suggests careful measurement; as a noun, it more typically referred to a kind of jacket).

Madre – As noted above, this is a curly-grained wood that was once used to make various vessels. (The word is extremely rare, even in French.)

Nef – This is an archaic word for a ship, but also referred to a container, usually extremely elegant and sometimes in the shape of a boat, which could hold various precious items, including, at the table, salt.

Parlement – This is almost the same word as the English *Parliament*, but the French institution was more a judicial than a legislative body.

Tables and utensils for meals

Table seating

Possidonius writes that the Celts took their meals seated on the ground on hay, having before them very low tables. According to Strabo, the Belgians ate, for the most part, laid out on sorts of beds. Finally, if one is to believe Diodorus of Sicily, the Gauls used, as seats, dog or wolf skins.

These testimonies of ancient Authors do not agree any more than many others, already previously cited. To reconcile them, it must be said that they concern different parts of Gaul. Nonetheless, if one must choose between the three Writers, I would most willingly trust Possidonius, who, having traveled among the Gauls, could have seen with his own eyes the custom in question. His testimony further agrees with that of Caesar who says that, in the army, the Gauls normally sat on hay.

Table beds

Such were, from the start, the Nation's first seats. Soon the Romans, established among them, taught them about the sort of beds which they used for their meals. In some regions, they might have adopted this custom; and in fact I find still some examples of this in the Fables of the XIIIth century, when they want to show us certain little pleasure parties.

One also reads in the *Monk of St. Gall*, the story of a magnificent meal which a Bishop gave to two Great-Officers of Charlemagne, whose favor he wanted to gain; and in which the Prelate was seated on feather cushions. But these examples are rare. From the start, the Gauls felt the inconvenience of a fashion as awkward as it was uncomfortable; they substituted, for beds, wooden seats and stools, on which they ate seated, and which they covered with a rug to make them softer.

Stools and benches

No doubt the Roman Generals conformed to this custom; above all when they felt they must cultivate the friendship of a people whom they might often need. Sulpice-Severus notes that when the Emperor Maxim admitted the Bishop St. Martin to his table, he put him on a stool beside him, *sellula justa Rexem posita*; and that the Empress, out of respect for the Saint, wanted herself to put the rug on his seat, *sellulam ipsa consternit*. In the agreement which was reached under Louis-the-Fat between Foulques, the Count of Anjou, Great-Senechal of the Crown, and the Gallerandes, who held this position since the King had stripped Foulques of it, it was set, according to Hugues de Cléry, that at the royal banquet, the day of the Monarch's coronation, Foulques would serve the first dish; and that while awaiting the moment to serve, a bench would be kept ready for him, which would be covered with a rug or some kind of cloth.

Stools, low stools were still used in Foulques' time; but they were only used at domestic meals. Whenever a great feast was given, the guests were seated on benches [*bancs*]; and from that comes our word *banquet*. Among Princes and Great-Lords, seats were only benches. We will read below of the table ceremonial of the Dukes of Burgundy, of which I will have a chance to speak, that among their Officers, there was one who carried the rug and the cushion for the Duke's bench.

Henri III introduced to the Court armchairs for his person, and folding chairs for his retinue; because this effeminate Prince busied himself on the throne with nothing but the search for pleasure. The Author of *Ile des Hermaphrodites* shows him to us this way, along with two of his Pretty Boys, *in chairs* (armchairs) *of velvet, made in a way called crushed. The rest of the troop had seats which opened and closed like a backwards waffle-iron.*

The use of benches endured, along with armchairs, until the last century. Régnier (Suite X) describing a festivity, says:

> At this point one washes [*the hands*]; and each by his rank
> Sits, in a chair, or on a bench,
> According to his merit, or his duty, or his position.

Tables

Among the different things which St. Remy, archbishop of Reims, left in his will to his heirs, he counts a silver table with figures, *tabula argenteam figuratum.*

In the Poetry of Fortunatus is mentioned a table, very artfully worked, on which a vine was represented. Charlemagne, says Eginhard, had three made in solid silver, which were *more impressive still for their work than for their material.*

These revealed not only a great and magnificent Prince, but an enlightened protector of the arts. The first showed Rome; the second, Constantinople; the third, the regions of the universe which were then known. Besides these three silver tables, Charles had another of gold. But, for this last, the historian does not tell us what it showed. (a)

a) Louis XIV, who resembled Charlemagne in so many ways, had also had executed, in the last century, a work of the same sort; which, with other infinitely precious objects, was exposed to public admiration in this vast room of the apartments in Versailles called the jewelry cabinet. It was a large table, eight and a half feet long, two and a half wide; which showed France, with all its details, according to the most recent astronomical observations. To imitate lakes and rivers, the Artist had formed his base of white marble; but at the same time, to show the provinces, he had embedded in this base pieces of marble of different colors, and cut exactly to the shape of our Provinces. He tried above all to make his mosaic most striking; in putting together, one after the other, the colors which mix most agreeably. For example, the Île-de-France was in light blue; the Orléanais, pale; Beauce, dead leaf; and Champagne, a porphyry red. Each Province bore its name in letters of gold, in capitals; and the main cities theirs in italics. In the north one saw the coast of England which corresponded to that of France. Finally, precision went so far as to show the capes and bays of the Kingdom. For a border there was a strip of blue marble, with its molding, then another

We read in the *Vies des Evêques de Ravenne*, by Agnellus, that Louis-the-Pious, when he succeeded his father the Emperor, also ordered a silver table, modeled on that of Charles, which showed Rome as one of his. Louis gave it to the Bishop of Ravenna, Martin. It is likely that this Prince, who was devout and entirely devoted to the Clergy, gave in the same way those of his father to other Prelates; from what Agnellus says, he only kept one.

I find further examples of silver tables until the last century. Mme de Sévigné (1689) speaking of the different people of the Court who, following Louis XIV's example, had their tableware taken to the mint [*to be melted*] says: *Mme de Chaulnes sent her table, with two ornate stands and her fine vermeil toilet.*

While the Nation ate seated on the ground, low tables sufficed; but as soon as it had adopted raised seats, it needed higher tables as well. The *Chronique manuscrite de Normandie* even tells in this regard a singular tale of Duke Robert, father of William the Conqueror. Robert had made a vow to make a pilgrimage to Jerusalem. In passing through Constantinople, he was quite struck to see that *the Emperor and all his people ate on the ground, that they had neither tables nor forms for seating.* The Greeks apparently followed in that the custom of all the Orient. For the Duke who was accustomed to another way, and could not conform to this one, he had made a table and chairs in the French style. He used the same in every place he went; and this furniture, adds the Historian, seemed so comfortable to the Emperor and his subjects, that they adopted it and *learned to make it.*

band of black marble, on which were marked the degrees of longitude and latitude.

I do not need, I think, to note that this work had nothing to with feasts, other than that it was called a table.

Rugs for meals

Although this fact seems to indicate a custom universally established among the French, there is nonetheless proof that that of eating on the ground was not entirely abolished there. I find an example of this towards the end of the XIth century, in the life of St. Arnoud, Bishop of Soissons. The Biographer, speaking of the dedication of a church which the saint was performing one day, says that he took his meal on the ground, having had a rug spread there; *expansis in terra taperibus*.

Hay and straw

Habit had also preserved in part the use of hay which the Gauls had used for seats. Only it was no longer used, as by them, to sit; but it was spread out beneath the table and in place for the party, in order to spare the feet of the guests the cold of the ground; as we do today with our woven rugs and carpets. Soon even as it was noticed that the smell of hay went to one's head, dry rushes and straw were substituted for it. Besides, these beds of straw were found to be so healthy and pleasant that similar ones were used in all the rooms of apartments. And above all among Great-Lords and Kings, where they were still more necessary, because of the vastness of the rooms which only had one fireplace.

Albérie-de-Trois-Fontaines, and the Chronique manuscrite de Normandie, says that when William, illegitimate son of Duke Robert, came into the world, the Midwife who received him held him a moment on the straw with which the room was strewn. The child having then grabbed with his hand a little of this straw, and the old woman having had trouble getting it away from him, the latter cried,:

faith, this child is starting early to conquer. The prophecy of the Child-birther was later verified; William, by his victories, earned this name of conqueror which she had given him in advance, and which his century confirmed to him.

In 1208, Philip-August ordered that whenever he left Paris, the straw used for his Bedroom, and even for all his Palace, would be given to the Hotel-Dieu of Paris. In 1373, the inhabitants of Aubervillier having asked Charles V to be released from the *droit de prise* (1), the King consented; on condition that they would provide annually to his Hotel forty wagon loads of straw, to that of the Queen twenty, and ten to that of the Dauphin. Twenty-five years after, the inhabitants of Chelles obtained the same favor from Charles VI for thirty wagon loads; in 1494, those of Houilles and of Carrières-St. Denis for four for each village; in 1406, those of Surêsnes for eight; and finally those of Chevailly for twelve.

Straw in Churches and Colleges

At midnight Mass on Christmas, straw was spread around the Church. The Schoolchildren in the College classes were seated only on straw. There was even a particular street where was sold that which they used for this purpose. It bore the name of *Foare,* a name which it bears still, and which came from this merchandise, which was so called in old speech. The Licensed Students in Philosophy were obliged to keep the Chancellor of the University supplied with this, and each paid him for that twenty-five sous.

a) Thus was called the obligation to which certain vassals were subject to provide horses and carriages for the King's voyages.

Greenery in festive places, in apartments and churches

As in winter, people tried to keep warm with straw, in summer they tried to keep cool with grass and leaves. The walls and fireplaces of apartments were also decorated with green boughs. *The Count of Foix*, says Froissart, *entered his bedroom which he found all bestrewn, and full of new and fresh greenery, and the surrounding walls all covered with green branches to make the place cool and sweet-smelling; because the weather and the air outside was marvelously hot.*

Brantôme recounts how Bonnivet lying, a certain night, with one of the Mistresses of François I, suddenly the King, who was not expected, came knocking at the door and alarmed our two lovers. *Then, the question was where the gallant could hide most safely. As it happened, it was the summer, branches and leaves had been put in the fireplace, as is done in France. By which the Lady advised him to jump into the fireplace, and hide in these leaves all in his nightshirt.*

Tavern-keeps themselves, for the pleasure of those who came to drink, also decorated the different rooms of their taverns this way; and often the municipal Bodies concerned themselves with maintenance of this custom. Among the diverse statutes of the city of Bordeaux, there is one, given in 1550 to Tavern-keeps, by which they are expressly directed to provide to drinkers *grass and straw*.

Finally, just as on Christmas, the floor of the church was covered with straw, it was covered with fragrant grasses on the day of the Assumption. The Abbé le Beuf (*Histoire du diocèse de Paris*), informs us that in the XIIIth century, it was the Priors of the Arch-Deaconate, named Josas, who, on this day, were obliged to furnish, each in his turn, greenery and flowers. In the XIVth this duty was no longer required; and normal grass sufficed, taken from the meadows of Gentilly. Jean, Duke of Berry, uncle of Charles VI, having fallen sick in Paris, gave his Hôtel of Nêle to the Chapter of Notre-Dame; on condition that, every year on the first of May, the Canons hold a procession with a green branch in hand, and that the church be strewn with green grass.

Tablecloth

I have spoken above of sculpted tables of gold and silver. I have spoken of another, on which the artists had painted a vine, and which, by the beauty of the work, merited being celebrated by Fortunatus. The Poet has left us an epigram on the latter, whose meaning is, *in seeing the grape, the guests drank the liquid.*

These words, in seeing the grape, seem to prove that a tablecloth was not then used. Certainly they had tables rich enough to expose to admiration. And in fact, would it not have been a mad luxury that these images, these sculptures, the mosaics of the highest price, be hidden under a cloth. Nonetheless, in the life of St. Eloy, who was a contemporary of Fortunatus, these are mentioned. Apparently, they were only used for ordinary tables of wood; but when a rich man, when a sovereign, could show off one, precious for its material or its workmanship, then undoubtedly it was served bare. Fortunatus himself, describing a voluptuous banquet, in which the place for the festivities was strewn with flowers, says: *the table, normally covered by a cloth, was by roses. The dishes there were set on flowers; and instead of a linen cloth, was preferred what flatters the sense of smell, and which covers it in the same way.*

What is more, the tablecloths were fluffy and velvety. That is how they are shown by Nigellus, author of a Poem on Louis-the-Pious,

Candida praeponunt niveis mantillia villis

[Set snowy white downy tablecloths]

I also think they were put on the table folded in half; and this conjecture, I base on an inventory of certain effects belonging to the Monastery of Fontanelle; which was inserted by the Abbot Ansegisus in the Constitution he made for this monastery at the start of the IXth century. One sees mentioned in it four tablecloths, each ten ells long by two wide; another, which was ten ells by three; and finally thirteen which were three ells wide. Surely linen of such a width would not have been made for the refectory tables if it was not folded in half. Perhaps further economy played some part in all this; and it was envisaged that after having soiled one side, one could then turn it on the other. Whatever the motive, it is sure that in the XIIth and XIIIth century, tablecloths were called *doubliers*. They bear no other name in the works of the Poets of this time.

Soon nonetheless something was changed in this custom. Instead of a tablecloth folded in half, it was preferred to put, on top of the first, a second, which was shorter, and that was removed with the last setting. Henri III, a Prince uniquely occupied, as I have said, with petty pleasures, wanted that on his table this upper tablecloth be artfully folded, like the ruffs then worn about the neck, and that it show drawings agreeable to the eye. According to the Author of *l'île des Hermaphrodites*, it was *folded in a certain way so that it closely resembled some rippling river which a light wind softly stirred. Because, among several small folds, one saw much bubbling. Under this tablecloth, there was another all of one color, which was shorter than the one on top.*

Further, there exist several books, written after this Prince, and which teach how to artfully fold napkins and tablecloths.

Napkins

Today when we use both the one and the other, we must think that their use is equally old. Yet that is not the case. I even think napkins to be rather modern. At least I have not found a single passage, quite positive and clear, where it is proved that formerly they were, like ours, used for the table. In truth, St. Angesis' Constitution for the Monastery of Fontanelle even mentions soft linen for wiping the hands, *lintea ad manus tergendas villosa;* but this does not refer to hand-wipers. I even find quite often the word napkins in the Prose writers and Poets of later centuries; above all when they describe the ceremonial practiced among Sovereigns and the Great; but these napkins were, either to be used by the Officers, the Prince's servants, or to wash and dry his hands and those of his guests, before and after the meal, or finally to cover their bread, their knife, etc. until the moment when they sat down at the table. No doubt were destined for this last use two napkins brocaded with gold of which there is question in an account of the Household of the Dukes of Burgundy for the year 1421; because one sees that they could not have been used to wipe the mouth and the hands. Probably the one and the other were wiped with the tablecloth; as is still done today by the English, who do not use napkins.

The custom of slicing the tablecloth

What confirms me in this opinion is the bizarre custom which was established in the middle of the time of Chivalry, when one wanted to insult someone, of sending a Herald, or King-at-arms, to cut the tablecloth in front of him, and turn over his bread. This was called slicing the tablecloth; and was above all done before those who had committed some base or cowardly act; *because it is not a pretty thing*, say the Statutes of the Heralds, *that a traitor be honored like another Knight or Gentleman.*

Although there is something ridiculous about such a custom to our eyes, one must admit that the motive which gave birth to it is infinitely respectable, since it tended to preserve honor. Thus, Alain Chartier gives as its originator one of our most famous heroes, Bertrand du Guesclin. This Bertrand, he says, *left in his time such a chiding in memory of discipline and chivalry that whatever noble behaved in a way that deserved reproach, someone came, as he was eating, to slice the tablecloth in front of him.* And in fact, one finds in our History, soon after the death of the Constable, an example of his custom, remarkable for its boldness.

Charles VI had at his table, on the day of the Epiphany, several illustrious guests, among whom was Guillaume de Hainaut, Count of Ostrevant. Suddenly a Herald came to slice the tablecloth in front of the Count, saying that a Prince who did not bear arms was not worthy of sitting at the King's table. Surprised, Guillaume responded that he bore the helmet, the lance, and the shield, like other Knights. "No, Sire, that cannot be, answered the oldest of the Heralds. You know that your great uncle was killed by the Frisons, and that still today his death remains unpunished. Certainly, if you owned arms, it would have been avenged long ago." This terrible lesson worked its effect. From that moment, the Count thought only of repairing his shame; and soon he managed it.

Manufacture at Rheims for table linen

Rheims was known for making table linen. Often even, so great was the reputation of the work of this manufacture, it was one of the gifts which the City gave to Sovereigns. When Charles VII made his entry there, it gave him flowered napkins. When Charles the Fifth passed through, while crossing France to go to Flanders, the municipal Body made him a present of the same sort, which was estimated at a thousand florins.

Damasked and worked linen

It is claimed that the art of damasking table linen is from the last century and that it is owed to the Grandorge family. The father, it is said, invented how to make, on cloth, flowers and squares; and in fact checkered napkins still bear the name of Grandorge. Richard his son made some with characters, animals, and other such figures; this is what we have called damasked linen, because of its resemblance to white *damask*. Finally, Michel, Richard's son, established several manufactories of damasked linen; which, it is added, made the use of it common in the Kingdom.

Nonetheless the richness of the present which the city of Rheims gave to Charles-Fifth, as seen above, the floral pattern, which the napkins bore with which it paid homage to Charles VII, allows no doubt that this was worked and damasked linen, and so that the invention in question, at least that of damasking, came before Grandorge. But what proves it undeniably is the testimony of the Author of the *l'île des Hermaphrodite*. In describing the table of Henry III, he specifically states that tablecloth was of *a prettily damasked linen.*

Whatever the case, if there was a time when we were the manufacturers of this linen, the factories of Flanders bit by bit brought ours down. We see from a letter of Mme de Maintenon (1682) that when she bought the land of this name, have wanted to establish there a manufactory of table linen, *worked like that of Tournai*, she was obliged to bring workers from Flanders, and that she *lured away twenty-five* (a).

(a) In browsing a manuscript which contained the transcript of the dissolution of the marriage of Louis XII, I encountered an extraordinary fact; it is the story of a torture applied to Sir de Vatan *with a napkin and water*. It is laid out in so obscure a manner that I found it impossible to understand; *but the napkin taken off of his face was*, says the manuscript, *redder than his suit, which was of crimson satin*. I leave it to the wisdom of my readers to decipher this enigma.

Torches and candlesticks

Torches and other such supports were not always used to illuminate the rooms for parties. The custom, under the first Race, at least among the Great, was to light the guests with candles held by servants. This is what is shown by a passage from Gregory de Tours about a French Lord, named Rauching, a man of atrocious cruelty, who during his meals, while his valet, as was the custom (*ut assolet*), held the candle before him, took pleasure, says the Historian, in letting burning wax fall on his legs.

Custom of lighting rooms for festivities with candles held in hands

Following this, although candle holders had been invented, the Great nonetheless kept the old custom; because this custom, in giving them the opportunity to display a numerous retinue, better satisfied their love for luxury. In the Account of the Household of Philip the Bold, Duke of Burgundy, one sees Serving-Valets, intended for this duty. When Froissart decries the magnificence of the Count de Foix, he tells us, *when he came from his room to sup in his hall, before him were twelve lit candles which twelve valets carried; and these twelve candles were before his table, which greatly lit the hall.*

At the Count's funeral, the same ceremonial was observed. *Twenty four great candles burned, continually and unceasingly, day and night, all around his body; which candles were held by forty-eight varlets, of which twenty-four watched all through the night and the other twenty-four all through the day.*

Servants were used for lighting even in the festivities and amusements of the Court. There was a masked ball where Charles VI came with several Lords, dressed like him as wild men, and attached one to the other by a chain. It was one of the torch-bearers who, through carelessness, set fire to the clothes of the Lords, burning them alive, and [which] would have consumed the King himself, without the presence of mind of a woman who saved the Monarch by wrapping him in her clothes. At the famous festivities which Louis XIV gave, in 1664, at Versailles, the gathering place was lit by an infinite number of chandeliers and girandoles; and further by two hundred Foot-Servants who held torches in their hands.

Hildebert, Author of the XIIth century, informs us in his *letters* that he had received as a present, from Mathilda, Queen of England, two golden candlesticks, sculpted, of remarkable workmanship; *opus preclarum coelatura*.

The Poets of the following century often mention candelabrae; but, by this word, they mean a torchère serving as a base for a very large torch. Besides, this is the meaning it had until the last century, where it came to mean a candle-holder with several branches.

Of all the candle-holders of which my work has presented me a description, the most remarkable by their size, by their form, and their richness are the two which the City of Paris gave in 1539 to Charles-Fifth, when he crossed France to punish the rebellious population of Ghent. In reference to the motto *plus ultra* which this Prince had taken, an ambitious motto which seemed to show in him the desire to carry his conquests beyond the two famous limits which Hercules had set as the limits of his own, each candle-holder showed a Hercules carrying off the columns, with the inscription *plus ultra*. It was further these columns which were intended to bear the candles. The Hercules was of silver; he was seven feet tall, and weighed four hundred marks.

Before this present, the City had given another like it to Queen Eleonor, sister of the same Emperor, and wife, in second marriage, to François I. These two torchères showed a pyramid, six feet high by two wide at its base. *And*, says Bochetel, *the two candle-holders were of old-fashioned work, with horns of abundance serving to hold sugar plums; and they were full of triumphs and dancing figures, sculpted in half work (half raised), the others sculpted in the round, with sayings in praise of the Queen.*

Bouchet (*Annales d'Aguitaine*) says that this work cost ten thousand francs.

Further, I do not think I need to point out that normally, among Great-Lords and Sovereigns, such ornaments were intended more to decorate showpieces than places of festivity. In the last century, the throne room at Versailles (a) had two torch stands, eight feet high; and four pedestal-tables six high, all of silver and garnished with girandoles.

Not all the candelabrae further were of silver. Louis XIV, at the start of his loves with la Vallière, sent one to this Young Lady which was of carved crystal. It cost two thousand louis, and was part of a piece of furniture of the same matter.

(a) It was so-called because of the silver throne that Colbert had had placed there for Louis XIV.

Candle [bougie]

Wax has always been burned in France. Candles made with this substance first bore in Latin the name of *cerei*; then, in French that of *cierges* which was derived from it. The first piece in which I recall having seen the term *bougie* is a Statute of Philip the Fair, 1313, in which he forbids mixing tallow with wax.

Candles with wicks

It is claimed that the art of threading the candle is very new and that it was brought to us from Venice towards the middle of the last century. The fact is not true. In 1357, after the battle of Poitiers and the capture of King Jean, the Provost of Merchants made a vow, in the name of the City of Paris, to give every year to the Virgin in the cathedral *a candle whose length would equal the circumference of the walls of the City* (a). One would agree, I think, that this could only be a candle with a wick. Besides, by the rules which Charles VI set in 1381 for the reception of a master Butcher, it is ordered that the new master shall pay, among other things, to the head of the Community a *rolled candle*.

Colored candles

De Serres informs us that, in his time (1600), candles were made of every color, yellow, green, red, marbled, etc. Still he adds that the use of this illumination was only suited to *Princes and Great-Lords;* and that the other ranks had to be satisfied with tallow candles.

(a) The offering actually took place every year until the troubles of the League, where it was sometimes interrupted. But finally, at the beginning of the last century, the City substituted for the candle a silver lamp which must burn without interruption, day and night, and which continues today.

Candle [chandelle]

The Chandlers [*Chandeliers*] are one of the oldest Communities of the Kingdom. From 1061, those of Paris had Statutes. Further, a XIIIth century Statute exists in their favor; which proves that then were known, as today, dipped and molded candles. But, other than selling this merchandise in shops, it was peddled as well in the streets; and further the wick was made half of cotton and half of thread, instead of our using today only cotton.

There were also different qualities of candles, according to the quality of tallow of which they were made. This is shown by an Order of Parlement (Sept. 22, 1565) which sets at three Tournois sous the pound of candle made with beef tallow; at 3 s[ous], 6 d[eniers] that made of sheep tallow; finally at 3 s. 4 d. that made of one-third beef tallow, and the other two-thirds of sheep.

According to the old etiquette of the Court of France, widowed Queens were condemned to spend the first six weeks of their widowhood, *without seeing other than candlelight.* Among the Officers of the Household of King Philip the Fair, of which the list will appear below, there were *three candle Valets.*

In Provinces where oil was made from walnuts, candles were also made, says Liébaut, with grape-pomace.

Oil candlesticks

The *Mémoires de l'Academie des Sciences* for 1755, 1760, 1763, mention lamps of a new invention which different individuals had presented to it for its approval. The base is that of an ordinary candlestick; but it is hollow in order to hold oil. Above rises a tin cylinder, also hollow, and bearing a small pump which makes the oil rise to the wick. These candlesticks were in fashion and were adopted by people in business. They were considered ingenious, of an agreeable form, and favorable to the view by the little hood which went with them, and which, without offending the eyes, brought all the light to a single point. But, as it was also found that they were dirty, difficult to clean when the oil had settled, requiring frequent repairs by the jamming of the spigots, they lost their reputation.

[Utensils]

Spoons

Among the works of charity performed by the Holy Queen Radegund, Fortunatus puts that of feeding, *with a spoon*, the blind and the poor whose infirmities made them unable to serve themselves. In the will of St. Remy, Archbishop of Rheims, are mentioned spoons, *both large and small.*

Knives and forks

The Celts, says Possidonius, *eat very uncleanly, seizing with their hands, like beasts, entire haunches of meat and tearing them apart with their teeth. If they come across a tough piece, they cut it with a little knife, which they always carry at their side.* There is no question here of forks; as can be seen; and there is no more mention of them in Writers well after Possidonius. The Romance of Partenopex de Blois, a work composed towards the end of the XIIth century, or at the start of the XIIIth, says:

tablecloths

Tables set and cloths,

Knives, salt cellars and spoons,

Cups, hanaps and bowls

Of gold and silver;

But he says nothing of forks. It will be seen below, in the description of a ceremonial observed at the table of Philip the Bold, Duke of Burgundy and son of King Jean, that when the Slicing Squire served the Duke some sliced morsels, he presented them to him with a knife. Finally nonetheless forks are mentioned in an inventory that Charles V had done of his silverware in 1379. Apparently until the time people began to use them, the knife was used to bring cut morsels to the mouth; as still do the English, who have for that knives whose blade is rounded and very wide at the end.

Under the first Kings of the third Race [*that is, the Capetians*], the knives of Beauvais were very famous. The *Chronique de Normandie* even tells the story of a Cutler of this City who having made a very handsome one and have come expressly to Rouen to give it to Duke Robert, son of Richard II, received from the Prince, for his reward, a considerable gift.

The piece *Proverbes* names as the most famous of its time (XIIIth century) the knives of Perigueux.

Under the reign of Henry IV, the knives at elegant tables were decorated, on the handle, with some bizarre figure, and above all with a head of a Chinese mandarin; which resulted in their being called knives of China. Régnier (satyre X) shows a quite ridiculous man,

.... *Whose scowling face*

Resembles of those Gods on Chinese knives.

Drinking vessels

Possidonius, describing how wine was served at the feasts of the Gauls, says that a servant brought to the crowd a sort of pot in earth or silver, filled with this liquid; and he adds that each dipped into it by turn. Apparently the individual vessels used to dip and drink were, although he does not say it, of the same material. This is at least more likely than what Strabo claims, when he states that the Gauls, like the Spaniards, drank in wax forms.

Horns

There were vessels which only belonged to the braves of the Nation, and which were especially theirs; such were the horns of the urus or wild bulls. My Readers will recall here what I said earlier [*in a separate chapter*] on the hunt of these fearsome animals The Gaul who had been lucky enough to kill one took its horns, which he kept, says Caesar, as testimony to his valor and intrepidity. He decorated them with rings of gold or silver; displayed them at home, and had his guests drink in them, all around, when he gave a feast.

Homer, and all the ancient Poets, show us the Heroes of antique times drinking from horns. According to Pliny, it was the custom of all the northern peoples; he could have said that of almost all the barbarian races; because it requires no more than instinct to drink from the hollow horn of a dead animal; and it required much thought and knowledge to have known how to work the earth and metals until they could be used as vessels. But what is remarkable is that, among the Barbarians who used horns, this custom came from ignorance and misery; and among our Fathers to the contrary it was the sign of courage.

The custom nonetheless endured in France centuries after the urus were destroyed, and so long after any honor was attached to the possession of their horns. Guillaume de Poitiers, describing a plenary Court which William the Conqueror held at Fécamp at Easter, shows us this Prince as having on his table vessels of gold and silver, *and drinking from horns which, at their two ends, were decorated with the same metals.* The famous tapestry which the wife of the Duke had made to transmit his conquests to posterity also shows many people using horns to drink. Finally, they are mentioned even in the Poets of the XIIth and the XIIIth century.

Sometimes even churches used them, but of a smaller sort, to hold the wine used to say Mass. The Monk Helgaud speaks of two cruets in this material, which King Robert gave to the church.

Human skulls

I hesitated some time before deciding whether I would tell here of an awful custom which existed among the Gauls; that of using, during their meals, cups made from human skulls. How could I not be allowed to doubt so horrible a fact! But they are reproached for it in so definite a manner by ancient Authors that one is obliged to believe it, cost what it will. Luckily, one can prove, by these same Authors, that it was particular to certain individuals and was not associated with the whole Nation. On the other hand, who would believe it, it was founded on ideas of glory so admirable in principle that in lamenting those who have abused it, one has trouble not excusing them for it.

The idea was established among the Gauls that, to be able to claim some honor in a battle, one had to have killed with one's own hand at least one enemy. Following this idea, when the Soldier had felled or defeated his adversary, he cut off his head to prove his victory; and came, after the fight, to bring this testimony of his valor to the feet of his General. These bloody trophies were set with ceremony in sacred places, they were hung from trees on the battlefield; they were attached to the walls or gates of towns. But, if in a battle, a brave had the luck to kill one of the enemy Generals, or even if he had killed a simple combatant in an individual challenge, then he was not obliged to present the head. It was left to him; and after what one has just read, it is easy to imagine what high esteem a people, brave to the point of madness, but still barbarian, must have attached to such a monument. The Warriors who possessed such sometimes consecrated them in a temple; and it is thus, according to Titus-Livy, that the skull of the Consul Posthumius, after having been chased with gold, was used among the Boyens for sacrifices. Others, says Strabo, embalmed these heads. If the families to whom they belonged wanted to buy them back, they demanded its weight in gold; and Diodorus of Sicily even states that several took pride in refusing them at this price. Another finally made of it a cup which he decorated with gold and silver, and from which, every time he gave a feast, he offered to drink to each of the principal guests in turn. I have said his principal guests; because not everybody had the right to this honor; to claim it, one had to have killed an enemy on a day of battle.

Dare I add that sometimes, but for another reason, the Gauls used for the same purpose the skulls of their dead parents. One shudders at this idea, and the hair rises on one's head; and yet this custom, which seems to us so abominable, was, for our Fathers, only a religious ceremony, dictated by respect and filial love. In presenting to their friends, during a meal, these sacred remains of the people who had been most dear to them, they recalled the memory of the latter; and even showed the attachment they had to them. As for us, we give over to decay and worms the cadavers of our dead parents; and it is thus that we satisfy the last duties of Nature. The Romans burned the bodies of theirs; the Egyptians embalmed them; the Gauls drank in their skulls; and these three Nations thought to satisfy the same duties as us. To spare his father the long pains of an incurable infirmity, the American Savage puts him to death; the Savagess of the coasts of the Orinoco smothers her newborn girl, to spare her the miserable fate to which the condition of her sex condemns her. Well then! Would one believe that this parricide Savage is a tender son; that this unnatural mother passionately loves her daughter! How many customs, in the history of nations, seem hideous to us, because we judge them by ours; and which we would perhaps call otherwise, if we were to look into the motive which established them and that which maintains them.

Cups

In the XIIIth century silver cups from Tours and the *hanaps* of Pontarlier were prized. The piece *Proverbes* counts them among the things of this time which were most prized.

Hanaps

The hanap differed from a cup in that it was mounted on a rather high base. It was a sort of chalice. These were in all sorts of material, earth, pottery, gold and silver. But the most prized of all were those of crystal; above all when were joined to these rare sculptures, precious stones, and other such ornaments. Bernier (*Histoire de Blois*) describes a hanap of this sort, which the Abbey of la Madeleine at Châteaudun possesses, and which tradition holds was one of the presents sent by the Sultan of Persia Aron to Charlemagne. It is of a considerable size and mounted on a silver base, which is enriched with threads of gold and enamel. Among the gifts which Charles the Bald gave the Abbey of St. Denis, and which is listed in the *Chroniques* of this monastery, there was a hanap which it was claimed had belonged to Solomon; which was *of pure gold, and fine emeralds, and garnets, so wonderfully worked that in all the Kingdoms of the world was never seen fine a work.*

Vessels for water and wine

To serve water and wine at the table, as they did not have, as I have said elsewhere, either carafes or bottles, different containers were invented which, by their shape or capacity, were called pots, ewers, hyders, barrels, *estamoies, justes,* pints, quarts, etc. When the Author of the *Dream of the Old Pilgrim* wants to show us the modesty of Philip de Valois at a feast he gave for the Kings of Navarre, Scotland, Bohema and Navarre, he says: *he had on his table only two gilded quarts, full of wine, a ewer, and his cup from which he drank; on the Royal dresser* (the buffet).

The bad taste of the time sometimes had these vessels made in the shapes of men, animals, and others still more bizarre. King Robert, says the Monk Helgaud, owned one of this sort, which represented a stag, and which had been given him by Richard, Duke of Normandy. The devout Monarch, after having used it some time in his banquets during solemn holidays, made a present of it to the church.

Nef, or Cadenas

One of these vessels whose shapes made them bizarre was that called, and still called, the *nef.* Its use was ancient; since, according to Glaber, it was one of the presents which this same Robert gave to the Emperor Henry during the conference they had by the Meuse.

The nef represented a ship; and it was from this that it took its name. It was intended to hold the salt cellar, the napkins, etc. of the Prince; because this fixture was only suited to Sovereigns and to very great Lords. To set it solidly, it was held up by mermaids, by lions; or simply by feet. Normally some particular ornament was added to it. We will see below, in the inventory of Charles V, a nef which, at each end, bore a serpent; and another which had a castle with towers.

The Author of the *Île des Hermaphrodites* informs us that under Henry III the nef was given the name of cadenas which it still bears.

Dressers

Formerly, among the people whose rank and quality allowed them dishes in gold or silver, the different principal pieces were shown on a buffet or credenza, which, from these pieces being set out [*dressées*] took the name of *dresser*. Given the retired life which Kings, Princes and powerful Lords then lived, shut up all year in their castles or palaces, and only opening their Court for certain festivities or great solemnities, this dresser was almost the only way they had to show their riches and their magnificence. Besides, the origin of such ostentation goes back, if you ask me, to the first age of the Monarchy.

Among the effects which, after the death of the Patrician Mummol, were seized at his home were found, besides a great quantity of tableware in gold and silver, fifteen large silver basins; of which one, among others, weighed one hundred seventy pounds. It is clear that so great and also so heavy a platter was only for display and could be of no use at the table. I say as much about this plate of solid gold, weighing fifty pounds, which Chilperic, King of Soissons, had made and encrusted with jewels, to *honor*, he said, *the Frankish Nation*, and from this silver plate, weighing seventy two pounds owned by St. Arnould, Bishop of Metz, and which he sold, according to the author of his life, to meet the needs of the poor.

What confirms my conjecture is that these enormous pieces were still more remarkable by how they were worked than by their material. When Sisenando, King of Spain, wanted to convince Dagobert to support him in his revolt, he promised him a plate of gold which weighed five hundred pounds; and which was *precious above all by the beauty of its work*. When Lothar, about to be attacked by his brothers at Aix-la-Chappelle, pillaged the treasure of his father, he broke up, say the *Annales de St. Bertin*, and distributed to his troops an immense silver platter, which represented, in relief, the universe with the course of the stars and the planets. Certainly one would agree that this work in relief was not made to bear a load of foods which would have crushed it. Without doubt, it was was only for show, like the other basins of which I have just spoken. Apparently it was set on a particular table, in the most visible spot in the room for the festivities. Later, instead of a single piece, people wanted to have several in different shapes; and from that came the origin of these tiered dressers, far more advantageous for displaying plate for show.

Normally it was only a table, covered with some precious cloth; *the dressers richly laden with stretched tapestries and drapes of gold*, says Mat. de Coucy. But these tables were cut in tiers and I have just said why. Monstrelet describing the magnificence of the Duke of Burgundy during his stay in Paris, reports that *in the room of his hotel where he ate was a square dresser in tiers; which dresser was covered and laden with tableware of silver and gold, very rich*.

Among Sovereigns who affected much magnificence, the buffets were of metal; and there were three; one for silverware, another for the gilded plate, and a third for the plate of gold. This is how it was at the meal that Charles V gave in the great hall of the palace for the Emperor Charles IV, his uncle; each of the three buffets had its dishes, its plates and its particular vessels; and each was of the same metal it bore.

From this fact, Villaret claimed in his *Histoire de France* that Charles was the first of our Kings who had a buffet. Philip de Valois, he says, giving a dinner for the Kings of Scotland, of Bohemia, of Navarre, and of Mayorca, only had at his table TWO GILDED QUARTS, FULL OF WINE, AND, ON THE DRESSER, A WINE SKIN IN WHICH WAS THE WINE OF THE KING.

I have reported, several pages above, the quote which Villaret reports here. But, if he had read it all, if he had consulted the very original from which it is taken, he would have seen that it proves precisely the opposite of what he claims; and that in the time of Philip, dressers, laden with dishes, were in use, since the author of the quote notes as a particular thing that that of the King only held a leather wineskin, *and had on it no vessels of gold or of silver, flagon or hyder.*

These dressers were so much a furnishing suited to Sovereigns that when the Emperor Charles IV, during his trip in France, went through Orleans, the city gave him a gilded one, estimated at eight thousand livres. The gift that the city of Paris presented in 1571 to Queen Elizabeth, queen of Charles IX, was in the same way a vermeil buffet.

The women of great quality, when they were lying in and began to receive visits, placed a dresser in their bedroom. But this dresser was not the same for all. A work, composed towards the end of the XVth century, and titled *les honneurs de la Cour*, informs us that there was an etiquette for this. *For the Countesses and great ladies*, the dresser bore a velvet dais with a back; but it could only have three tiers. On the tiers, one was to place large cups, pots, flagons of silver; and on the console, two comfet-boxes [*for candies*], two silver candle-holders, or other such pieces similar to those on the tiers. The younger sons of the Knight-Bannerets could give their wives lying in a dresser with two tiers. Finally for the *well-born* women, but without titles, it had to be without tiers.

Next to the buffet, a small table was set, covered with a white cloth, and intended to hold the hypocras and the wine which was given to those who came to visit the expectant mother. The table had particular cups; because one was not allowed, to drink, to use one of those from the buffet. No other than a woman could offer wine or sugar plums. If the person who came to visit was a Princess, it was not to her directly that the comfet-box was offered, but to the lady who followed her; in order that the latter offer it to her.

The Author is careful to note that at the lying-in of Isabelle of Bourbon, daughter-in-law of the Duke of Burgundy, Philip, the etiquette was different. The dresser then had four tiers, instead of three. The dais, instead of being of velvet, was of crimson cloth of gold, edged with black velvet. Finally, the console, instead of holding two comfet-boxes, held three, which were of gold and inlaid with stones.

Although metal buffets were one of the furnishings of Sovereigns, the Great-Lords nonetheless, and people of standing, allowed themselves similar ones. "What sort of dishes do Bishops have, the Author of *Vigiles de Charles VII* asks himself. They have handsome and large dressers of gold and of silver, pots, flagons, etc. – And the poor? – The poor have the bread left on the table."

In the XVIth century, dressers lost their old name to take that of buffets. Under the Reign of Henry III, the Court called them credenzas, from an Italian name with the same meaning. *Formerly this was called the buffet; then it was named the credenza*, says the Author of the *île des Hermaphrodites.*

Imitating the Great, the burghers, and down to the common folk, made themselves dressers. Eustache Deschamps, a Poet who died towards 1410, listing in a long satire which he wrote against marriage, all the inconveniences brought by a woman one marries, says: *you need pints, pots, ewers, a dresser with lots of plate, if not of silver, at least of lead and tin.* We still see remnants of this old custom in the buffet-armoires of our dining rooms; and above all in these little tables on which our peasants neatly arrange their tin dishware, and a few copper basins which which they are careful to polish for the great holidays of the year.

Aside from the silver dishware with which the dressers where garnished, they were also sometimes decorated with flowers. Among the rents which the inhabitants of Chaillot were obliged to pay annually to the Abbey of St. Germain des Près, there were two large bouquets and a half-dozen small ones, *to put on the dresser.*

One of the small particular rooms which Louis XIV intended, in the Chateau of Versailles, for the collations which he gave on certain days of amusement, was called the *salon of buffets*; and in fact it held three of them; two for the liquids, the sherberts, and the fruit waters; and the third for the hot drinks, like chocolate and coffee. This last was set between the two others, and had as an ornament a large silver shell.

At the meal which the Prince of Condé gave in 1680 for the wedding of Mlle. de Blois, illegitimate daughter of Louis XIV, with the Prince of

Conti, the buffet, says the *Mercure Galant*, was decorated with basins, vessels, tubs, and numerous other works of silver and gilded vermeil, *sculpted*. On the two sides had been set, as decoration, two orange trees in their boxes.

Flowing fountains

In the century of Deschamps, the Sovereigns and the Great-Lords sometimes had at their meals flowing fountains; which provided, during the meal, the wine, the hypocras, and the other drinks which were drunk there. Normally at the same time rosewater, or some other sweet-smelling water, flowed to perfume the room. I would be inclined to think that, from the XIIIth century, were known in France these sorts of hydraulic mechanisms. I see at least an example in the voyage of Rubruquis, one of the Monks which Pope Innocent IV and King St. Louis sent to the Khan of the Tartars to try to convert him. Rubruquis informs us that he found in Tartary a Parisian Silversmith, named Guillaume Boucher, who having established himself with the Khan, had made him one of these fountains of which he had no doubt brought the idea from Paris. Boucher's was a large mechanism since it was made of three thousand marks of silver. Besides, as it may make familiar the taste and the industry of the XIIIth century, as besides it belongs to us through the artist who constructed it, I flatter myself that the description of it will be read with pleasure.

It consisted of a large silver tree, at the feet of which were four lions, of the same metal, which each spewed a liquid of a different sort; one of wine; the other, mare's milk (a drink much sought by the Tartars); the third, of ball (a sort of hydromel); the fourth finally of rice brandy.

These liquids came to the lions' mouths by pipes hidden in the tree's trunk; and the pipes ended, by the branches, in a neighboring room where they were filled. At the top of the tree was a silver angel, holding in his hand a trumpet, and who, by means of a spring, brought it to his mouth to play. The Silversmith's original intention was at first to use for this several bellows; but not having succeeded in this way, he had come up with the idea of piercing, under the floor, a route to the foot of the tree, to adapt to this a tube whose end was at the mouth of the angel, and to hide a man there, who, in breathing into the tube, made the trumpet sound.

Thus, when the Khan gave a feast, and one of the guests asked for drink, the Sommelier yelled to the angel to give the signal. Then the angel brought the trumpet to his mouth; the man hidden under the tree made it sound; at once, from the room outside, the conducting tubes were filled; and the four liquids were received in silver vessels which the sommelier went to take to the table.

During the festivities which Philip the Fair gave in 1313 in Paris, when he made his children Knights, a fountain was also seen from which flowed wine. It was guarded by leopards, lions, and other ferocious animals; and the liquids which flowed from it formed a pool in which swam swans and mermaids.

These fountains were given different forms, according to the invention of the artist, or the whim of he who had ordered them. Thus, for example, at a feast, of which one will read the description [*in a later chapter*], and which was given by Philip the Good, Duke of Burgundy, there were towers, from whose tops fell a rain of orangeade; a statue of a woman, whose breasts provided hypocras; and another of a child, *who peed rose-water.* The Romance of Tirant-le-Blanc shows us, in a similar circumstance, a similar spectacle. Aside from a statue of a woman, from whose breasts flowed a liquid, there was further *a young woman, made of enameled gold, She was naked, and held her hands lowered and pressed against her body as if to cover herself. From under her hands came a fountain of delicious wine, which was received in a transparent vessel.*

Fountains with several different liquids were adopted by Municipalities. They put such in the principal streets and crossroads during public celebrations and above all for the entries of Kings and Queens. When Isabeau of Bavaria made hers into Paris, each crossroads, according to des Ursins, had *a fountain which sprayed water, wine and milk.* J. Chartier says that at the entry of Charles VII, these sorts were seen in the rue St. Denis, facing the Filles-Dieu; *one of the tubes sprayed milk, the other red wine, the other white wine, and the other clear water, with people all around; holding silver cups, to give all who passed by to drink, if they cared to drink, and whichever they wanted.*

In the last century, the use of flowing fountains was still the custom in meals. The *Mercure galant* (March 1681), describing a feast which eight gentlemen gave in Marseille during the carnival, says that the buffet there had a jet of orange blossom water which played all through the dinner.

Earthen pottery

Of all the materials which Man has tried to put to use to make himself table and kitchen utensils, the most anciently, the most universally in use without doubt is earth. Long before he knew how to dig into mountains to discover metals there, clay must have presented itself to his view; the effect of rains would have shown him that one can soften and shape it; and it would not have been hard after that for him to harden it in the sun or fire.

We have seen above that the Gauls, in their meals, used earthen vessels. There still exists at Francheville in the Lyonnais a factory of this pottery, that a tradition of the region claims to precede the Roman invasion. Paris had several established on the mount St. Geneviéve. When in 1757 and 1758, this terrain was dug up to set the foundations for the new church dedicated to the Saint, about a hundred and fifty pits were found, of different shapes and sizes, formerly dug by the Potters who lived on the mount. Some still held fragments of their pottery; and those who saw them say that they were very beautiful.

There were also Potters in the streets of the Capital; because the pestilence caused by their ovens having provoked, at different times, the complaints of neighboring houses, the Chatelet in 1486, and the Parlement in 1497, handed down, one a Sentence, the other an Order, by which these artisans were to take their workshops outside the walls.

Faience

It is striking that our Fathers knowing how to work clay had not thought to give it this fine and brilliant coating which transforms it into faience. In the XVth century, and in the XVIth above all, almost all the faience used in the Kingdom came from Italy, and notably from Faenza, and from Castel–Durante, places which had several famous factories of this. It was not thought that our Provinces could provide anything like it.

Works of Palissy

The first who tried it was Palissy. Chance, in 1555, had made fall into his hands a cup of this material, perfectly enameled, and of a rare beauty. At this sight, his imagination was enflamed; he wanted to divine the secret that he admired, and to manage to imitate it, if it was possible. Palissy, as is known, was a man of genius, but a simple worker without a fortune, who after having traveled a part of France, settled in Saintes; where, burdened with a wife and several children, he earned his living painting images on vellum, and figures on glass. Everything conspired against the success of his effort; because, besides the considerable expenses which it required and which his misery forbade him, he knew nothing either of the furnaces, nor of the enamels and earths which he was going to be obliged to use. Thus, to use his own words, he began his operations *like a man feeling about in shadows*, each day trying a new material, or a different method; sometimes using Potters' furnaces, sometimes those of Glaziers; then ending by constructing one himself with his own hands. But it is in his writings that one must seek these truly picturesque and touching details, where he shows all he suffered of pains and labors. Tormented within his household by his wife, harassed outside it by his neighbors who called him a madman, reduced to such distress that one day he was obliged to give his worker's clothes in payment, and another, to burn the floorboards and the tables of his house to finish the heating of his furnace, one sees him, for sixteen whole years, persisting stubbornly against all obstacles, and, as soon as he had earned a little money, taking up his labors again with an invincible courage.

Finally, he succeeded. He managed to work, to enamel earth as he pleased. The greatest Lords of the Court, the King himself, and the Queen-Mother, employed his talents; and it is then that he took the bizarre title of *worker of earth and rustic figulines* [sic] *of the King*. Today still one sees a few of his works in several Chateaux of France, at Nêle in Picardy, at Reux in Normandy, at Madrid in the bois de Boulogne, and elsewhere. Ecouen above-all, where the Constable made him work a great deal, offers from him different curious pieces; and among others, an entire pave stone in enameled tiles which, by the vivacity of its colors and its variety, causes the eye this pleasure, mixed with surprise, which is easier to feel than to express.

But what Palissy particularly liked to make, as his writings prove, that in which he excelled, was reptiles to decorate gardens in his fashion; because this man, truly unique, had imagined gardens in the taste of those that today we call "English". He decorated with them grottoes, cascades, fountains and artificial streams, on the banks of which he put lizards, frogs, etc. enameled in natural colors. He even made fish of this sort, which, through the water, seemed like true fish.

But all these discoveries only concerned the magnificence of a few Greats. Although Palissy also sometimes made plates and bowls decorated with figures of animals, nonetheless he only used his talents to beautify gardens, doorways, or apartments in chateaus. Besides he always kept his methods secret. Thus can one say that if he worked for his fortune and his glory, he did nothing for the craft which he had worked out. We had no more faience than before.

Things remained so for some time. But finally, it is said, an Italian, expert in this art, having come to France with the retinue of the Duke de Nevers, and having discovered, near the city of this name, earth like that used at Faenza, he made there, it is claimed, these same sorts of works, which he called faience, from the name of the Italian city; and which soon, inspiring the emulation of our other cities, led to similar factories there.

Faience factories established by Henry IV

That is one of those tales one finds repeated everywhere and which are regarded as historical facts. To destroy it, it is enough to cite what de Thou reports on this subject, in 1603. Speaking of various establishments which Henry IV created for the prosperity of France, the Historian says: *he built manufactories for faience, white as painted, in several places in the Kingdom; at Paris, at NEVERS, at Brissambourg in Saintonge; and what was made in these different workshops was as beautiful as the faience gotten from Italy.*

As for the name of this sort of pottery, it is not at all to *Faenza* that we owe it, as is claimed; but to the little town of *Fayence*, in Provence, in the Diocesis of Fréjus; one of the first places in the Kingdom where work had been done in this style, and whose workshops already had some reputation before the establishments of Henry IV (a).

Repairing faience

Sixty years ago a way was found in Paris to get some benefit from broken faience, in rejoining its fragments with staples of wire. This invention, which some of my Readers will find ridiculous that I mention here, but that, despite its little importance, I nonetheless feel obliged to cite because it is an object of economy, is due to a certain Delile, from the village of Montjoie in lower Normandy. Called and employed for his talent in most kitchens, his example turned several other people of his kind towards this little branch of industry. The Faience-makers whose sale they harmed tried to forbid it to them; and brought a suit against them. But the iniquitous greed of the merchants gave way, and the profession of faience-repairers was declared free.

Madre

Our old poets of the XIIth and XIIIth centuries often mention vessels of *madre*; and they speak of it as a rare and precious thing. I do not know what this material is [*curly-grained wood, in fact jc*]. Maybe it was porcelain; because trade could procure some for us, by way of the Levant, as it procured us spices. Still, as one sometimes sees madre counted among the utensils of peasants, inn-keepers and common folk, as further there was great and small madre, probably this last should be understood as faience, or some such composition; either because the secret of it was known in France or because it was brought from abroad.

(a) Mézeray describing the success which Lesdiguieres had in Provence, when he entered there in 1592 with his troops, says: *Fayence more renowned for the earthen vessels which are made there than for its size or its importance;... and five or six other fortified places showed him little resistance.*

Porcelain

Porcelain is yet another of these objects of luxury which we owe to Asia. For a long time, Europe only used what it got there; and used it without knowing its make-up. Pancirole, in the XVIth century, claims in his book *Des choses perdues et inventées*, that it was made of plaster, egg whites and scales from seashells (a) buried underground for twenty-four years; so *that a worker who undertook this profession only worked for his heirs*. But finally it was known that porcelain was a pottery, or faience, finer than the others.

Saxon porcelain

In the last century, the Baron of Boëticher, Chemist at the Court of the Elector of Saxony, August, even discovered this secret and made it at home in Europe. He was looking for a new combination of earths which could provide him crucibles capable of resisting the most violent fire. He in fact found one, from which he obtained a paste so beautiful and as perfect as that from which Japan made its porcelain. The Elector to whom he communicated his secret profited from it to establish at Meissen, near Dresden, a factory, from which came works so perfect they were worthy of Sovereigns.

(a) A letter which appeared in the *Mercure* (July 1678) fights the idea that porcelain was made with egg shells. Still, Haudicet de Blancourt, (*Art de la verrerie*, 1593), in teaching the methods for making it, still makes his paste of white seashells, reduced to powder, and kneaded with gummed water, and with melted chalk. "When the vessel is formed, he says, a polisher of silver or copper is used to polish it after it has been left to dry, and varnished with enamel, it is given a first baking; then the colors are put on it and it is put in the oven a second time." The author concedes nonetheless that, instead of seashells, one can use a white earth, powdered and used the same way.

The news of this discovery and of its successes resounded all through Europe. All the Chemists, and in particular the Chemists of Germany, were stung by the desire to discover Boëticher's formula, or at least to find one of their own. Several of these last managed this. In several regions of Germany, one saw as a result Princes build, as they wished, porcelain manufactories. Several have since acquired the greatest reputation, and can be compared to the factory of Meissen. Among these are those of Vienna, of Berlin, of Frankendal, and that which the duke of Virtemberg set up at Louisburg, near Stuttgart.

The English too had their factories; but instead of trying, like the Germans, to discover the secret of China, they thought to do better by getting directly from this country, using their vessels, the very materials used to make porcelain; an ill-conceived expedient, which they soon abandoned.

Among us, during all the last century, luxury and fashion made porcelain worth an infinite price. It will be seen by descriptions of several festivities which I will describe further on that the Greats then gave neither a feast nor a collation in which they did not display a certain number of select pieces of it. At Court, it was admitted on the table together with dishes of gold and silver. Loret (*Muse historique*) describes a feast, *truly royal*, which Cardinal Mazarin gave in 1653, and in which this Minister

Feasted two Kings, feasted two Queens,

With plates of silver, of porcelain,

Discovery made in France

Luxury had accredited in proportion this foreign production among the class of the rich. Every year, the Nation used considerable sums for it, and its industry, so ingenious for many other subjects, paid this heavy tribute indifferently, without dreaming that it could be freed of it. Thus, Boëticher's discovery which caused such a sensation in Germany only produced a minor one among us. There was nonetheless one of the members of our Academy of Sciences, named Tschirnhausen, who sought, and found, like him, a composition of earths analogous to that of the Chinese or Japanese. He confided the secret to his colleague, Homberg, with this bizarre condition, that it would not be made public until after his death. Homberg only kept his word too well, because he died without having shared it.

Establishment of a factory at St. Cloud

Nonetheless, in 1697, the Masters Chicaneau built at St. Cloud a porcelain manufactory. The novelty of such an enterprise, so near the Court, could not fail to inspire curiosity. At the end of December, 1699, the Dutchess of Burgundy came to visit. Monsieur went there with Madame; which raised the suspicion that the Government was trying to bring the establishment some prestige. But, despite the glamor of these brilliant visits, which were carefully promoted in the *Mercure* of the following month, it had no reputation; apparently because the true principles of the new craft were not yet known.

The first writing which gave some sure ideas of this was a Memoir published in 1717 on the methods used by the Chinese. The Author was a French Jesuit named d'Entrecolles, a Missionary to China. But, since d'Entrecolles announced that the two principal materials of the

Chinese workers were Kaolin and Petunse, no doubt people were scared off by these foreign names; it was not believed that France could provide earths which were so called in Nankin; and the Missionary's Memoir remained without effect. Except that, some of our Faience-makers made, in crude porcelain, sleeves for table knives. Cane knobs were even made in Paris which were called, from their shape, crow's beaks [*bec-de-corbin*], and which were very much in fashion, because they were decorated with gold and made pretty with colors; but all these silly novelties did not produced porcelain.

Réaumur's experiments

Finally, Réaumur started to work on this subject. He had known that the F. d'Entrecolles, in sending his Memoir to France had also sent there petunse and kaolin. He had obtained samples of them; analyzed these, and declared that the Kingdom had earths analogous to these, and capable of replacing them. Such was the subject of the two Memoirs which the Author published in his turn, and which appear among those of the Academy of Sciences, 1727 and 1729. Experience has since shown that he was right. Still, he had made a mistake in his choice; and further, he had set, as a certain principle, a known error, that is that porcelain is only a vitrification. Thus his work resulted in no real result; although the analysis, by which he had begun to operate, should have led him to some interesting discovery.

Chantilly porcelain

The Duke of Orleans, Regent, had thought also, following d'Entrecolles' Memoir, to make porcelain. Because few people in France knew Chemistry as well as this Prince. He in fact established several workshops for it; and soon the new craft could have boasted of rapid progress, had its protector been as constant in his tastes as he was enlightened in his projects. But the love of pleasure which invincibly ruled him, the habitual dissipation in which he lived, the little discipline of his too ardent character, finally his death which came soon after, left the work to languish. M. the Duke, in succeeding to his position, adopted his enterprise. He gathered workers and established them at Chantilly, where, in his turn, he built a manufactory which had some light success, and which continued to enjoy it after the death of the Duke.

Sèvres porcelain

Things remained so until 1740. Then two brothers, named du Bois, in charge at Chantilly of the paste and the baking of porcelains, left the manufactory and came to offer their services to M. de Fulvy. The du Bois were dissolute and lost in debt; M. de Fulvy was known to them by several fruitless efforts, undertaken to make porcelain; and they flattered themselves that in promising him their so-called secrets, they would find in him the restorer of their fortunes. In fact, he welcomed them as favorably as they could have hoped, and even obtained for them the special protection of his brother, M. Orry, Comptroller-General of Finance. The latter placed their workshops in the chateau of Vincennes and granted them all the necessary spaces. After all, it was shameful that foreign countries already possessed, for a long time, famous manufactories of this sort, and that France, this country of luxury and industry, still did not have a single one. Nonetheless, the du Bois, in less than three years, having dissipated sixty thousand francs, without teaching anything essential, because they always wanted to make themselves necessary, M. de Fulvy, weary, talked of driving them away.

He went yet again to see the fruit of his lost advances when a certain Gravant, a simple worker, but an intelligent and skilled man who had profited from the frequent drunken bouts of the du Bois to learn or guess their methods, offered him in good faith the knowledge which he had gained. This offer revived hope. He sent away the du Bois, gave the running of the manufactory to Gravant, bought from a certain Caillat the secret of colors, lured away several workers from Chantilly and made passionate efforts. Although this time they were made honestly, the costs nonetheless so far exceeded the income that M. de Fulvy seeing his enterprise become a burden to him, was obliged to turn to his brother.

This Minister formed a Company of eight associates, to whom he granted an exclusive privilege for twenty years, with the use of all the spaces necessary to them in the Chateau of Vincennes. To procure gilded pieces in porcelain, the associates concluded a private agreement with B. Hippolyte, a Benedictine, who had the secret of applying gold on paste. Each of them put down thirty thousand francs; and, with this help, the manufactory began to live.

The Minister what is more had a particular interest in it. Often he came to visit it. He himself, with the intent of perfecting the different efforts, named Master Mathieu, Enameler to the King, to inspect the painting and the gilding (a); Master Duplessis, to direct the Molders, the Turners and the Repairmen; and Master Hellot, Chemist, from the Academy of Sciences, (b) to improve the making of the paste. With such means, a few successes could be noted; but the death of M. Orry, in 1747, that of M. de Fulvy in 1751, suddenly upset the projects.

(a) In 1749, M. Bachelier was named to this position.

(b) In 1753, the King gave M. Macquet as an aide to M. Hellot; and, three years later, when M. Hellot died, M. Macquet's aide was M. de Monsigny.

Still the associates did not lose courage. They were skillful enough to interest Mme. de Pompadour in their enterprise, and obtained from this Lady that she convince the King to take this manufactory under his Royal protection. This is what happened in 1753. His Majesty even consented to pay a third of the costs required by expenses. Then everything turned around. By the choice of Artists employed in the workshops, one saw coming out of it works of which several would be admired by posterity as masterpieces. Pleasant ornaments, brilliant colors, perfect forms and painting, in a word everything which this exquisite grace which is that of French Artists can conceive of, the new porcelain brought together. Nonetheless people of a severe taste sometimes criticized it for too much color, too much gold, several of these careful details with which it was sought to imitate silverwork without having its precision, strange and tormented forms, finally painted subjects which were studied and mannered, because several were copied from Boucher. Besides, it could never be more than an object of ostentation. Glass–like, fragile, likely to break at the least heat, it was the worst porcelain in the universe, as it was the most beautiful.

This last defect lay in its paste, which was only a frit, that is, a vitrifiable earth which, in the furnaces, had not been heated to the point of glass. Chance subsequently presented something to substitute for this imperfect composition. It was a very white clay which an Apothecary of Bordeaux, named Vilaris, discovered in Limousin, and which was used only for porcelains called hard. The old frit nonetheless was not completely put aside. It was still used for pieces of pure display which bear fine and select painting, and which as a result one was obliged to retouch and fire several times.

The first important work which the factory produced was a service for the King. It was, in 1754, displayed in Paris to public admiration. The satisfaction which His Majesty showed in it led the associates to bring their workshops closer to his sight. For that, they bought at Sèvres, on the road to Versailles, the house which the Musician Lully had lived in, and in 1756, they took all their work there. From this moment, in fact, the King seemed to take a livelier interest in this factory. He honored it several times with his presence; and, four years, later, even reimbursed the associates in order to become its only owner. The reputation of the works which it produced grew more each day; they became a present worthy of crowned heads. In 1757, the King sent a service of them to the Queen-Empress. When M. de S. Priest left for his embassy to Constantinople, he was tasked with taking one to the Great-Lord. The King of Denmark, the King of Sweden, when passing through France, had a similar gift. Under the present Reign, the same presents have been made. The Emperor received one during his stay in Paris. This year of 1782, a magnificent toilette in porcelain was given to the Countess of the North. Often His Majesty gratifies with a service foreign Ambassadors who are at his Court, and even those of his own who leave for foreign Courts. Three years ago the Empress of Russia ordered an entire one for herself. Each plate was worth as much as 240 livres, and represented on its outline five heads of illustrious people, drawn from antique models. Finally, it was noted that before 1760, France received annually, from foreign countries, 300,000 liv. worth of porcelain; and then it began to sell it abroad for 300,000.

Nonetheless, Sèvres porcelain, despite its justly earned reputation, despite the discovery of clay in Limousin, still does not have the solidity of that imagined by M. the Count of Lauraguais. The latter, presented by the Author, in 1766, to the Academy of Sciences of which he is a member, resisted the most violent reverberatory fire. He reddened it in an ordinary fire, and threw in after cold water or vinegar, without its changing in the least. If it had the same finesse and the same whiteness as that of China, it would have made it forgotten.

For fifteen years, in different parts of the Kingdom, and particularly around Paris, a considerable quantity of manufactories has risen up which almost all offer a porcelain capable of bearing fire. It would be desirable that this charming tableware, the most agreeable of all, as well as the healthiest, proliferated enough in France to reign alone in our festivities. What a seducing look it adds to the foods confided to it; and who of us, in seeing this silverware with which the rich load their tables, has not said under their breath a thousand times what once the Peruvians said to the Spanish, when the latter gave them crystal vessels in exchange for gold: "What? Can it be that a dirty, dull metal makes you despise such brilliant and beautiful works?" But the wish of which we speak can only take place when, by less expensive processes, the price of porcelain has been brought down to that which our faience currently has. Until that moment, it will only be a luxury furnishing, forbidden to the greatest part of the Nation.

Glass porcelain

If, in a vessel, one sought only goodness, cleanliness, and the lowest price, there is none which would deserve to be compared to that conceived by Réaumur. It is no more than ordinary glass made into porcelain. What is more, ordinary glass, the most common and the most crude, is clean in it. It is white, goes on fire, and bears all the trial of boiling water. First it was criticized for small holes with which it was riddled. But no doubt the Glaziers found a way to correct this defect; because I have seen cups, sugar bowls, and other works of this sort, which were as brilliant and whole as the most beautiful porcelain. Although in Paris there are several Fayence-makers who sell that in question, still it is little known; and yet for how many purposes would it be useful, even in the imperfect state in which it first was.

Crystal glass / glassworks under the first Race

French glasswork, under the first Race, had some reputation. We read in the life of S. Benedict Bissop, Abbot of a Monastery in England, and deceased towards 690, that after building his abbey, he came to France to find workers to build him *a stone church*, and Glaziers, to *enclose with windows* its church, its refectory, and its cloister; because this last sort of fabrication was not known in Great Britain; *vitri factores artifices Brittannicis eatenus incognitos*. The workers whom Benedict brought taught their craft to the English, says the Author.

This is not the moment to discuss our window glass. This subject will have its place elsewhere. I will satisfy myself with saying here that our Glass-works then made cups, plates, and other table vessels in glass. Fortunatus, in a piece addressed to Queen Radegund, describes a feast in which each sort of food was served in a different material: the meats were on silver plates; the vegetables on marble plates; the poultry, *on glass plates*; the fruit in painted baskets; and the milk in black pottery shaped like stewpots. St, Benedict of Aniane used a glass chalice to say Mass, writes the Author of his life (a). Finally, among the things which St. Ansegesis, Abbot of Fontenelles and a contemporary of Benedict, gave to the Monastery before becoming a Monk, there was a *glass hanap, and two glass cups, decorated with gold.*

(a) The inconveniences which could result from so fragile a material, if by chance the chalice happened to break during the sacrament, led to their being forbidden by a Council of Tribur, held in 895. But the Council's interdiction was not observed. One sees still, in the XIth century, the Emperor Henry send to Richard, Archbishop of Verdun, an onyx chalice, and another of crystal. A charter of Count Eccard speaks of a sapphire chalice.

French XIVth century glass

Here is what was made of this sort in the XIVth century. The list is found in a charter granted in 1338 by Humbert, Dauphin of the Viennois, in favor of a certain Guionet. The Dauphin leaves to Guionet part of the forest of Chambarant, to establish a Glass-works there; but on condition that the latter provide him, every year, for his Household, a hundred dozen of bell-shaped glasses; twelve dozen small wide-mouthed glasses; twelve dozen hanaps or stemmed cups; twelve of amphorae; thirty six of urinals; twelve of large bowls; six of plates; six of plates without rims; twelve of pots; twelve of ewers; five of small vessels called *gottesles*; one of salt cellars; twenty of lamps; six of candle-holders; one of large cups; one of small barrels; finally a large nef, and large butts for transporting wine. (One sees that in all this there is no question of bottles.)

In the XVIth

In the XVth and XVIth century, Murrano, in the Venitian State, having become famous for its manufactories of mirrors, crystal, and ordinary glass items, our Glass-works declined; and we used only in this style what came from Italy. Henry II, to keep in his Kingdom the money which this object of trade made flow out of it, drew to France a certain Italian, named Theseo Mutio, who possessed the secret of this foreign glass, and set him up at Saint-Germain-en-Laye, where Mutio raised up a factory in imitation of those of Venice. But the crystalline glasses of Murano were made, says Bélon (*Observations sur les singularités trouvées en Grèce, en Asie*) with ashes from the country, and with Tessin pebbles. Well, the French could not procure either these pebbles, nor these ashes. They substituted then for those sand from Etampes, which luckily was found to be better. As for ashes, as they did not have any as good as those of Murano, they used glasswort from Provence.

In the XVIIth

Besides, the St. Germain Glass-works only survived so long as the King protected them. Soon the misfortune of the civil wars wiped them out. But, in 1603, Henry IV, the restorer of France, established others at Paris and Nevers. Nonetheless, although he established them at great cost, according to de Thou, they only languished. Richelieu's stormy and despotic administration held such concerns in contempt. Colbert, whom the spirit of Louis XIV too often turned more towards glamorous than useful things, created mirror manufactories, and paid little attention to items in glass which were not luxurious. Those of mirrors earned some merit; but the others fell bit by bit into such deterioration that in 1759 the Academy of Sciences proposed a prize for bringing to this both economy and perfection.

In the XVIIIth

The anointed Author was M. Bosc d'Antic; and his Memoir deserved this all the more in that since its publication, our Glass-works have turned around. A number have taken shape which make white glass, both for windows and for the table; and, what must be noted above all, is that white glass is no more expensive today than green glass was in 1760.

Our Glass-works nonetheless, although perfecting themselves each day, are still far from the point they could reach. If one is to trust the

Author, we only have, who would believe it, three of them in France where good bottles are made; Sevres, near Paris; Folembray, in the forest of Coucy; and Anor in the Hainaut. Saxony, Bohemia, Franconia, the Palatinate, etc provide us annually, for considerable sums, table crystal, flagons, carafes, glasses, goblets, and other such objects. England itself, whose manufactories only have been known for twenty years, sold us, before the war interrupted its trade with us, many drinking glasses, and above all many chandeliers and lanterns; because it particularly excels in the composition of the paste of chandeliers, in the art of polishing them, of sculpting them, of arranging the pieces, and so that of making them produce from candles all the dancing of lights, all the sparkling reflections which charm our eyes.

Precious stones

We have seen above onyx and sapphire used for chalices. These same precious stones were used for table vessels, as well as all others that are transparent. We read in the life of St. Fridolin the story of one of these vessels, *vas lapidem, vitrei coloris, auro gemmis que mirabiliter ornatum*, which were accidentally broken at Clovis' table, which the Saint miraculously restored. Louis the Fat had a nef of root of emerald [*prime d'émeraude*]; but having given it in surety, and not having been able to take it back for ten whole years, Suger asked and obtained permission to buy it for the Monastery of St. Denis, of which he was Abbot. It is even one of those things which he cites in the work which we have from him on the improvements, the goods and embellishments which he made to this Convent during his administration.

Crystal

In the inventory of Charles V's tableware, one finds ewers, pots, cups and goblets in crystal (a).

Mother of pearl, jasper, marble

In that of the Dauphin Humbert II, there is mention of a goblet of mother of pearl and of a jasper cup.

Finally, in the life of St. Sulpice, Bishop of Bourges, one reads that the Saint never wanted to use silver vessels, but that his were in earth, in wood, or *in marble.*

(a) The curious can go see in the King's Garde-Meuble a rather large number of works of this sort, which Time has handed down to us despite their fragility, and which are as remarkable by the eccentricity of their forms as by the finish of their work. I considered showing them here engraved. But, when I asked about the different pieces of this collection, the people responsible for their care, told me that they had not on any information or notes; that most were brought abroad, and had only been in the King's possession for a short time. I then renounced my project, for fear of presenting as national monuments which are not such at all.

[Metals]

One readily understands that materials such as mother of pearl, jasper and crystal could only suit Sovereigns or very great Lords. Marble itself, although it was for a Bishop a fixture of humility, was too expensive for the common folk. This class of men needs more solid, less costly utensils; and this is what common metals provided.

Tin and lead

Although, according to Pliny, according to Strabo, Possidonius, and Diodorus of Sicily, Gaul had mines of tin and lead, although independently of the tin which its mines produced, it still got a great deal from England, nonetheless these Authors do not inform us that it made tableware with these two metals. They were used for that later; I have provided proof of that above in speaking of the Dressers of the common folk; and I could still cite others. Today we must be all the more surprised by this use, at least for lead, in that this metal tends to dissolve, with heat, into fat and oily substances. Well, it is known that dissolved lead, taken internally, is a true poison. The tin from our mines, itself, is not without danger, because it contains lead. Luckily the use of this tableware is disappearing daily. It has even been abandoned in most religious Houses, Seminaries, and Colleges, in favor of faience which, aside from being healthy, is further, over time, more economical.

In 1741, a master Kémerlin presented to the Academy of Sciences a tin of his making which he claimed could be employed usefully and without danger in our kitchens. After a severe analysis and very careful experiments, the Academy declared that the new composition, though it contained an alloy, although less fine than the tin of Cornwall, still had nothing dangerous for the health, and that it was even harder to melt than normal tin.

Two years later, another person presented two others of these, which because of their fine color he called *simil-argent* ["like silver"], as Renti has called his red brass *simil-or* ["like gold"]. These were both rejected by the Academy, and judged imperfect.

Copper

The copper of Gaul's mines was admired in Rome, but, to flatter Livia, Augustus' wife, the Romans, say Pliny, changed its name from Gallic copper and gave it that of *Livien*.

Several Gauls, says Possidonius, used copper for their table plates.

Tinning

More than one fatal experience no doubt taught them the unfortunate property of this metal of becoming a mortal poison through contact with acids, even by lingering liquids. It was probably to protect themselves from this that they thought of covering it inside with a layer of tin and lead, alloyed together. This composition is what we call tinning. Pliny admits that its invention is owed to the Gauls.; but did the Gauls use it as a protection against verdigris, or only as an object of luxury for various decorations on their furnishings? The Naturalist does not say. Nonetheless, what makes me think they first began to tin their kitchen equipment, is that, later, says the Author, "they invented another tinning in silver for the bits of their horses, for their harnesses, and for their cars. This was even so brilliant, and they so excelled in the art of applying it, continues the Historian, that one could hardly tell it from their normal silver."

We still use the first; because against all good sense, we have always continued to use copper in our kitchens. Nonetheless, accidents caused by this treacherous metal have so multiplied, and sometimes even caused talk, that the government finally forbade it, two or three years ago, to certain merchants, and notably to milk-sellers. All those who, from neighboring villages, bring milk to Paris no longer have any but wooden or tin vessels. In many houses, the masters wanted to have only such equipment. But most Cooks to whom an express order had not been given have refused to adopt it; because not being very thick and thus allowing too strong a hold to the fire, it requires a great deal of attention to avoid burning the stews. It follows from all this that the man of the people who, to prepare his food, uses earthenware; that the burgher who can have plated iron equipment; then have an advantage over the rich man, since at least they do not run the risk of poisoning themselves.

In truth, Master Déranton, Clockmaker in Paris, recently found a way to use copper with impunity; in lining the inside of casseroles or terrines of this metal with a cover of fine silver, so amalgamated with it that it forms a single body with it. His secret, approved by the Academy of Science, confirmed by a Decision of Parlement, 1769, which granted the Author a privilege, is an ingenious thing, and even economical; but nonetheless these are still economies which are not those of everyone. Thus those who continue to use copper in their kitchen equipment continue to use the normal plating.

Nonetheless, a certain lady Dumazis has just invented one which, more expensive in truth than the old one, at least has none of its dangers. This is made, as is known, of tin and lead; and that of the lady Dumazis is of tin and silver. Her invention was approved by the Academy of Sciences and announced in the Journal de Paris, February 13, 1782.

Varnished sheet iron

One can count in the class of platings the art of varnishing sheet iron, which was found a few years ago. This secret has been known, for a very long time, in the Levant. It is used there for certain types of vessels, and particularly those which, like tea pots and coffee pots, were intended to hold boiling liquids. The varnish with which they are covered resists the effect of fire.

Italy, England and France sought successively to guess the secret of this strange composition. The English alone managed it entirely. At least, they are the only ones who have united at once in their varnish brilliance and solidity. Theirs is so shiny that it reflects objects like a mirror. In Paris, a Master Clément, Painter-Varnisher, announced one for which he established a manufactory in 1768. But, as the works which came from it lacked the fine polish of those of England and the Levant, it had no success. A Jeweler, named Framery, took it over from him. Without boasting of the beauty of his, he gave them neatness and taste, rather pleasant paintings in blue, red, gold, coverings of adventurine, japanned lacquer, false lacquer (a),

(a) The secret of making lacquer is no more than a century old in Paris.
   Haudicourt de Blancourt says as much in his *Art de la Verrerie*, 1697.
   It is, he says, *a very new Craft; and it is only very recently that it has
   been practiced in Paris, having been brought to us from Venice.*

false porcelain. As for the works produced by this new factory, these were handkerchief holders, *bougeoirs*, baskets, toiletries; and for table centerpieces, platters, trays, buckets for chilling wine, buckets for glasses intended for liqueurs, etc.

Silver

At the Nation's origin, it was easy for opulent people to have, for their kitchen and for the table, tableware and kitchenware of silver; Gaul then possessed abundant and very rich mines. In fact, Dion, Manilius, Joseph and most ancient Authors show us this country as fertile in precious metals. We know that it is with the gold of the Gauls that Caesar subjugated Rome; as it was with the iron of the Romans that he had subjugated the Gauls.

Mines of Gaul

If we are to believe Diodorus, Gaul produced no silver (a); but gold was so abundant there that it was enough, to become rich, to gather what had been carried by torrents and streams. Ausonius, in his poetry, gives to the Tarn the epithet *Aurifer*; and today still the small streams which come down from the Pyrenees roll, with their sand, a few flecks of gold of which the search provides a branch of industry and trade to the peasants of these regions. Pliny cites a gold mine in the place he calls Albicracense, whose minerals only contained a thirty-sixth part of silver; which is to say it gave gold of 23 31/32 karats, while that which comes out purified from our crucibles is only of twenty-four. Athenaeus speaks of our gold mines. Strabo says there were some in Aquitaine, near Dax; in the Cevennes and the Pyrenees.

(a) According to Strabo, the Gévaudan and the Rouergue had silver mines.

But, although one found this metal almost at the earth's surface, nonetheless one had to dig for it; which contradicts Diodorus who claims that the Gauls took no more trouble than to gather gold from the beds of their streams.

From the multitude, the abundance and the richness of our mines, one will not be in the least surprised by the immense quantity of gold and silver, worked, or minted, which existed in Gaul. When Toulouse was given over to pillage by the Consul Caepio, the booty of this city amounted, in gold alone, says Justin, to a hundred and ten thousand pounds weight (a).

Mining undertaken since the XVth century

In 1471, Louis XI was finally persuaded that the Kingdom possessed a great quantity of gold and silver mines. The Monarch, as a result, published a very favorable declaration, capable of encouraging those who wanted to undertake their exploitation. But try as he might to encourage, the digs and the works were fruitless. In vain François I and Henry II confirmed and extended the favors promised by Louis; theirs produced no more. Finally, the good Henry IV, among the diverse projects which he formed for the improvement of France, when he felt himself secure on his throne, having restarted that of mining, he entrusted the execution of his views to several experienced

---

(a) Strabo makes it understood that it was not at Toulouse itself that these treasures were found; but in a neighboring lake, where for a long time the Gauls, by superstition, had the custom of throwing a great deal of gold and silver. The enterprise of drying this lake was put up for auction; and those to whom it was adjudicated found even millstones in solid silver. This tale makes more credible the fact of the enormous sums which were the victor's prize.

people. The latter, after digs and careful research in different regions of the Kingdom, came to report their findings. Here is, according to the *Chronologie septennaire*, what they consisted of:

> In the Pyrenees, talc and copper, gold and silver;
> In the mountains of Foix, jet, and precious stones;
> Near Carcassone, silver;
> In the Cevennes, tin and lead;
> In Auvergne, iron;
> At Annonai, lead;
> In the Lyonnais, near St. Martin, gold and silver;
> In Normandy, silver and tin;
> In Brie and in Picardy, marcassites of gold, and of silver;

The talk which such an announcement caused at Court suddenly awoke all the Courtesans' greed. These words *gold and silver* had struck their ears; they imagined inexhaustible treasures, and used as they could reputation and intrigue to obtain an interest or a position in the new enterprises. The Great-Squire Bellegarde had himself given the Superintendence; Ruzé, Secretary of State, the position of Lieutenant-General; Bellingan, first Personal Valet, that of Comptroller-General, etc. It was all about who could get soonest, or get more. But this was to take beforehand the fruits of a tree which was still only a seed. Their greed was deceived. These mines from which they expected so many riches required considerable costs to operate and proved to be so poor that de Thou advised abandoning them. De Thou saw rightly; and all the efforts made since, of the same sort, have proved that he was right.

It is not the less true, as has just been read, that our same mines formerly produced a great deal; and that precious metals were very common in Gaul. Most Gallic Captains, and even certain soldiers, wore bracelets, collars and chains of gold. The Latin Authors offer proof of this in a thousand places. Manlius was only nicknamed *Torquatus* because he took one of these collars from a Gaul he had killed in single combat. It has formerly been seen that the Nation decorated with circles of gold and silver the horns and the vessels in which it drank; it has been seen that in its festivities wine was brought in a large bucket of earth or silver. The platters used for meats were, says Possidonius, of the same material.

Abundance of silverwork in France under the first Race

So much magnificence was to be wiped out in part by the pillaging of the Romans, and by those of the Barbarians, Huns, Franks, Burgundians, Visigoths, etc. who swarmed or devastated Gaul. Still vestiges of it remained in the following centuries. Witness these enormous platters, these tables in gold and silver, mentioned above; witness this chair of solid gold which St. Eloy made by order of Clothar II, and this throne of the same matter which Dagobert ordered from him. Count Leudast having come to Paris, he amused himself, says Gregory de Tours, in going about the merchants' boutiques, examining the silver plate and jewels which they displayed: *argentum pensat, atque diversa ornamenta propicit*. One reads in the life of St. Voué that, for a time, he was fed by the charity of an Abbess of Soissons. But, one day when she sent him his dinner on a silver plate, a poor man having come to ask alms from the Saint, Voué, who had nothing to give, gave his share, which the beggar carried off with the plate. The Monk of St. Gall tells the story of a meal which a Bishop gave to two Officers of Charlemagne to win their benevolence; and in which one was served on gold and silver plate, and in vessels encrusted with stones. In the will made in 813 by Dadila, Great-Lord of Septimania, he left to the poor, among other things, vessels of gold which he had received from his master. Finally, St. Sulpice, Bishop of Bourges, only used at his table utensils of earth, wood or of marble; *and never of silver.* This is a remark by the Author of this life to prove the sanctity of the Prelate; but this remark itself shows that silver was a common enough luxury.

This luxury lasted until the ravages of the Normans who, by the enormous ransoms which they took successively from France, ended by draining it. The fall of the Carolingian Race, the fearful anarchy, and all the internal wars which followed it further added to its misfortunes.

Still, such is the constitutional vigor of this so surprising Nation, such is its activity, that, despite so many defeats, a few intervals of repose were enough for it to regain its strength. Already it began to show some opulence, when suddenly it felt this fever of the Crusades which led it over time to swallow up itself its inhabitants and a part of its new opulence. It no longer had however these abundant mines which once made it so powerful and so rich. Its only resource was the fertility of its territory, its industry, and its trade; and these resources will be inexhaustible forever. Hardly had the Overseas wars finished, already one of our old Historians in verse reproached the Officers of Philip the Fair for numerous plate in gold and silver.

> They have great plate,
>
> …. Pot, and bowls
>
> Of gold and silver, fine and handsome,
>
> Various cups and *hennas**
>
> *hanaps

Kings' statutes on the subject of silver and gold plate

This luxury, what is more, was not exclusive only to Officers of the Prince. It spread through all the Nation, since Philip himself published, at various times, four different Statutes to repress it. By the first, in 1294, he forbids all those of his subjects who do not possess six thousand livres tournois of income to have plate of gold or silver for eating or drinking; and so he orders whomever does not have this revenue to carry theirs to the Mint. In the second, published eight years later, no one is excepted. Those who were by the first were obliged to send half their plate to the Mint. In 1319, he forbids Silversmiths to make any. Finally, in 1313, he orders disposing of a tenth part of what one has.

More moderate than he, his son Charles the Fair contented himself with forbidding any piece that weighed over a mark. But Philip de Valois renewed the Statute of 1310; and the fabrication of any type of silver whatever was forbidden to the Silversmiths (a).

(a) Louis XII, in 1596, forbid them every piece of large plate, and only allowed them sundry works like salt-cellars or spoons; or at most cups and pots whose weight did not exceed three marks. But, as the French chose to buy their silver plate in foreign countries, the Silversmiths complained that all this contraband was ruining them; and the Monarch, in 1636, had to revoke his Statute. Louis XIII, in 1636, published a similar one which he was obliged to annul two years later. Finally, Louis XIV, in 1672, having forbidden making and selling pitchers, *buckets, basins and other silver vessels serving to decorate buffets, andirons, silver burners, braziers, branched candle-holders, girandoles, mirror plates, caskets, tables, pedestal table, bread baskets, baskets, vessels, urns, and other utensils in solid silver, all plate and all silverwork exceeding eight mark s, all basins exceeding twelve, and any plate of gold whatsoever*; having renewed this Statute in in 1687, he modified it also in 89. Although he added to the first interdiction that of *desks, prongs ,fire or fireplace furnishings, arms, plaques, torch-holders, small chests,*

These regulations had the success one might expect. One can judge this by this Gascon Squire, of whom Froissart speaks, whom he met in an inn of Ortais, and who had himself followed by plate of gold and silver, with which *he and his people* were served. Eustache Deschamps, shows us the Canons under Charles VI having some in gilded silver. In the discourse which Juvénel des Ursins, Archbishop of Rheims gave to the Estates of Tours in 1468 against the different abuses which afflicted the Kingdom, he says that there was presently no one in France *who does not want to eat on kitchen plate of silver.* The Monks of St. Denis had, in the refectory, cups of this metal. They gave them to the Count of Dunois, at a moment when the latter had difficulties paying some mutinous troops. Dunois got about forty marks from it. Finally, when Louis XI, in one of these passing fevers of devotion which calmed for an instant his vices and his cruelties, came up with the project of making a shrine for the relics of St. Fiacre, and of enclosing those of St. Martin in a grill-work of from sixteen to

orange cases, flower pots, toilet squares, ring boxes, stewpots, pie plates, casseroles, of whatever weight, flasks or bottles weighing more than eight mark s, torches weighing more than four; nonetheless he allowed, under this new rule, pieces which he had forbidden under the two others; these were plates of four mark s each, saucers of five, ewers of seven, sugar bowls of three, salt cellars, pepper shakers, and other sundry table utensils which did not exceed two. He confirmed all this with an Edict of March 1700. Only, he forbade in this last, *olio pots, tiered plates for serving fruit and table centerpieces*, furnishings which probably had been invented since 1659.

seventeen thousand marks of silver (a), he named Commissioners, says Monstrelet (b), *to go take and seize all the plate to be found in Paris and other cities*. But although he paid reasonably everything he had taken, many people nonetheless hid theirs; so that, says the Historian, when one went to a feast or a wedding, *places where people were accustomed to go, one only saw handsome glasses and ewers of fern-ash-glass.*

Silverwork in the camps and the armies

I end here my references, although it would be easy to bring them up to our century. But to those one has just read, I will ask permission to add one still, taken among another class of people, to answer a famous Author of our time. He claims that silver was only introduced in our armies towards the middle of the last century, and that it was for the first time by a Marshal of France, one of the Generals of Louis XIV. To this assertion, it suffices to oppose the testimony of Montluc. In the time when this Officer was Colonel-General of Infantry, he had occasion, one day, to give the Duke de Guise, his General, an impromptu dinner. The meal, despite the little time he had to prepare

(a) In 1522, on the advice of the Superintendent Semblancay, Francois I, had this grill-work removed and made from it a coin on which was shown a trellis, as if to recall its origin. The common folk only saw in this trellis a sacrilegious irony, which only made it find such a profanation still more scandalous. They regarded as a divine punishment the misfortunes which befell the King several years later, made prisoner at Pavia, and to the Superintendent, hung at Montfaucon.

(b) It is not in Monstrelet; it is in the Chronicle which is printed after it which serves as a supplement that one finds this fact. But so far, in order to avoid copying a long title, I have put, as I will do from now on, under the name of the first Historian what belongs to the second.

it, was nonetheless so well ordered that the Duke, surprised, spoke of it to the King, and asked the Colonel what he could do to oblige him in his turn. "I asked him, says Montluc, to get the King to give me money *to have some silver plate; because nothing was lacking but that.*" But if this table lacked only silver plate, silver was then one of the ordinary things that all Officers of a certain rank put on theirs.

What if I were to cite the example of du Guesclin, who had golden plate, with a nef of the same metal *decorated with very beautiful rich stones*. It is true that du Guesclin had received the one and the other as a present from the King of Spain; and that, later, in a moment of distress, he sold them to pay his troops. But, since the brave Constable had accepted them, and since he used them, it must be that military honor and discipline did not find itself in the least compromised by that.

Presents of silverwork given by Kings to Ambassadors

Kings then used to give presents of plate, and above all to foreign Ambassadors who came to negotiate with them. In 1451, Charles VI gave those of Flanders *one hundred marks of silver in gilded plate, of which some were very pretty*. Sixty years later other Ambassadors from the same country received from Louis XI, says Monstrelet, *thirty thousand crowns of the sun, and largely of silver plate*. Finally, those that the Emperor Maximilian sent to Louis XII, recounting the way in which they were received, say: *The King sent to our lodgings fine, great and honorable presents, all in silver plate, chains of gold and otherwise in coin, even to the least of your messengers.*

Commines reports a dispatch sent to Louis XI, in which one reads, that *it is the custom to give plate to Ambassadors, be they friend or foe*. Still, Bassompierre writes that when an Ambassador had not received what he asked, he did not accept the gift.

Silver given as gifts to well-placed people

In all times, individuals have used such gifts to win the favor of people they needed. We read in the *Miracles de S. Benoît* that, in 653, the Monks of Fleury having a trial at Chateau-Landon, the Abbot sent the Judge two silver vessels, fairly heavy; *non contemnendi ponderis*. Geoffroy, Prior of Vigeois, tells in his Chronicle how in 1138, Eustorge, Bishop of Limoges, having died, two competitors presented themselves at once to succeed him; that is Gérard, his nephew, and a certain Amlard. Each of them was chosen on his side by a different faction; but Gérard, a more skillful intriguer, went to Rome to confirm his election. Not having succeeded, he returned a second time, laden with presents; invited to eat the principal leaders of the Pontifical Court, and put in front of each guests different well-worked metal vessels; *vasa diversa operati metalli*. That was not all. He attended the Mass given by the Pope; and offered, for the peace of his uncle's soul, he said, another vessel filled with pieces of gold. The means worked; Gérard's nomination was confirmed by the Pope.

Given to Churches

For the same motive, silver was given to the Church, as *ex votos*, when one wanted to obtain some grace from God. One of the Officers of King Pepin, says the *Miracles de S. Denis*, having miraculously been beaten and broken in body for having let his horse graze in a field which belonged to this Monastery, the King came to give, in reparations, a silver vessel to the Church and to ask for his servant's health.

Often pious people left in their wills, or even gave, during their lifetimes, some pieces of their silver to Monasteries or Cathedrals. Such was, among a thousand others, Léodebald (623) who, dying, left to the Convent of St. Pierre a golden bowl and two gilded bowls, all three from *Marseille*; such was Ermentrude who left in the same way, towards 700, to the Abbey of St. Vincent of Paris, ten silver spoons; Hélinard, Archbishop of Lyon, in the Xth century, who gave to the Monastery of St. Benignus of Dijon, of which he had been Abbot, all his plate; Guillaume, Count of Astarac, who had rebuilt in 983 the church of the Convent of Simone, destroyed by the Saracens, gave at the same time as a present eight vessels in silver, weighing ninety pounds; finally, Gérard, Bishop of Angoulême, who in 1135, left in his will to his church, a hundred volumes (a), and a great deal of silver for the divine Service.

No one is unaware of the generous and selfless procedure of the Chartreux of the Grande-Chartreuse. Guillaume II, Count of Nevers, had sent them silverwork; *argentea, scyphes videlicet et feutros pretii plurimi.* They sent it back to him, says Guibert de Nogent, and asked in preference that he give them parchment to copy books (b).

(a) *L'Histoire des Evêques et des Comtes d'Angoulême* gives the list of the Authors of this precious legacy. Since it might be of interest to some of my Readers, I will copy it. *Scripta Gregorii, Augustini, Ambrosii, Hilarii, Isidori, Cyriani, Gregorii Nazianzeni; Origenis, Hieronimi, Bruni, Bedae, Rabani, Boëtii, Paschasii, Sidonis, Historiam parvam et Historiam Julii-Caesariis, Scrupti Tullii.*

(b) The Count retired among them in 1147, and took orders there.

Convent treasures

These plates further, these vessels, this gift plate was not at all used by the Monks. They were kept in a particular place with other curiosities, jewels and reliquaries; and a treasure was made up of them which was shown on certain days, and at certain hours, to outsiders, as the Monastery of St. Denis still does, and several others. The life of St. Angilbert, Abbot of St. Riquier, who died in 814, witnesses that this Abbey possessed a jar, and two silver ewers with their basins; a key, a purse, and a golden baldric; thirteen gilded hanaps; a knife decorated with gold and stones; a silver inkwell, enriched with gold; etc, etc.

One sees in the life of St. Angesis that the Convent of Fontenelles possessed similar riches.

Kings' treasures

Kings themselves followed in this the taste of the times. They also had a treasure, partially made up of plate, both old and new. A foreign Prince came among them and the first spectacle presented him was that of all this magnificence. This is what Charles V did, when the Emperor, his uncle, came to France to visit him; and in fact few Kings, as will be seen further on, could boast of being as rich in this way as Charles.

Often, on days of great ceremony, the Royal treasure was shown publicly to the admiration of the subjects. *Christmas Eve*, says Monstrelet, *the King went to hold court in the Palace, where he celebrated the holiday most solemnly. … and there was brought a very great number of vessels of gold and silver, which were usually used for the high holidays.* François I, at the birth of Princess Elizabeth, his daughter, gave, in the courtyard of the Chateau of Fontainebleau, a similar spectacle. There was seen a vast theater, bedecked with leaves, and covered, as a sky, with a blue veil sprinkled with golden stars. From the theater rose a pyramid, with several faces, and of nine levels, where had been skillfully set an immense quantity of plate, of vessels and other pieces. Their number was such, says the *Trésor des merveilles de Fontainebleau*, that one thought to see there *the choice of all the buffets of all the Princes of Europe*. In effect everything had been brought together there of this sort owned by the different Royal Houses. That is not all. In order that the spectators might better admire the merits of the different pieces set out for their eyes, there were Officers, with express orders from the King, to make known their history. They told *how some of these rare pieces had been brought to France by the Emperor Charlemagne; as others had been sent to him by several Kings; and so other singularities, of which not one was modern, but all antique.*

Thus then the Kings formed for themselves, in each of their Palaces or Chateaus, a little treasure of curiosities; and this treasure, they made it especially of pieces of plate which they had inherited, from age to age, from the Princes their predecessors. This will be proven again when I present the inventory of Charles V.

Presents of silver made to Kings by their subjects

What is more, it was not difficult for our Kings to amass what was needed to one day satisfy the ostentation of their descendants. The custom then was that their subjects sometimes present to the Sovereigns gifts of plate. This same inventory which I have just announced will prove it. A piece given by the Bishop of Noyons will be seen there, another given as a New Year's gift by the sire of Chevreuse. The *Chronique de Normandie*, to give us an idea of the liberality of Duke Robert, son of Richard II, tells how one day a Knight, who came to pay him homage, having presented him a *juste* of gold, Robert took it and gave it away at once. Another day when someone came in the same way to bring him a golden cup, he similarly made a present of it.

By municipalities

On certain occasions, Municipalities often gave these sorts of gifts. Among those which King Jean received from various people, during the brief appearance he made in Paris while he was prisoner in England, one thousand marks of silver plate were counted which were presented to him by the Capital. When Isabeau of Bavaria, wife of Charles VI, made her entry into the same city, the Municipal Body offered to the King, to the Queen and to the Duchess of Touraine, sister-in-law of the King, similar presents. Those for the Duchess were a nef, two large pots, six other smaller pots, two comfet-boxes, two large platters, two dozen cups and saucers, two salt cellars in gold and in silver; those of the Queen, a nef, two salt cellars, two comfet-boxes, two large flagons, six pots, six soaking-troughs, twelve lamps, and two basins. Everything was in gold, except for the last two articles, and weighed three hundred marks. The King's plate only weighed one hundred fifty; it was entirely of gold. It consisted of four pots, six soaking-troughs, and six platters. Each of the three offerings was brought to the palace on a litter covered with a transparent veil, so that they could be seen by passers-by. Froissart speaks of this only with admiration; and he reports the fact as witness of the great power of the Parisians.

Towns of the Provinces often prided themselves on the same liberality on such occasions. Vienne, at the entry of Charles VI, gave him gilded plate. Amiens, at that of Queen Charlotte in 1463, gave two comfet-boxes weighing twenty marks.

By monasteries

Not even Abbots of Convents failed to sometimes, and for holiday gifts especially, give their offering. We have a letter from Pascase Radbert, Abbot of Corbie, written to Charles the Bald to beg the Monarch to accept the work which he sent him on the Eucharist and to receive at the same time, harnesses for horses, clothing ornaments, presents in gold and silver, and vessels of different sorts.

Louis the Young, ready to leave for the Holy Land, having demanded a considerable sum from the Monastery of Fleury, and the Monks not finding themselves in a state to provide it, the Abbot sent to the King, to make up for it, several pieces of silver, among them two candelabras weighing thirty marks.

By conquered cities

In time of war, villages vanquished by force of arms used this means to buy themselves out of pillage. That of Metz, in a similar circumstance, gave Charles V, says Monstrelet, two hundred thousand crowns, and *certain gifts of gilded plate.*

By Sovereigns to their allies

Finally, sovereigns gave such gifts among themselves. Sully tells how in 1600, the Duke of Savoy sent to King Henry IV, for a holiday gift, two large basins, and crystal vessels. The Duke and the Monarch then were negotiating for the Marquisat of Saluces. At the marriage of

Richard, King of England, with the daughter of Charles VI, the father-in-law and the son-in-law, as I have noted elsewhere, sent each other plate. Richard gave a very fine vessel for drinking *cervoise [like beer]*, and another vessel as well for putting water in; both encrusted with precious stones; and Charles, a very fine cup, a comfet-box, a ewer, a nef, and two large pots; all equally encrusted with jewels. The two pots were worth, according to Juvénel, around twenty thousand crowns.

The Abbé Véli (*Histoire de France*) writes that at the marriage of St. Louis *one saw, as a very rare thing, two gold spoons, with a cup of the same material which came to twenty crowns*. Everything we have just read until now destroys the Historian's assertion. In all the time of the Monarchy, and even from its origin, our Kings had plate of precious metal. I will only cite one or two examples taken from the *Chroniques de S. Denis*. St. Germain, Bishop of Paris, came one day to beg for the poor the piety of Childebert. The latter gave him a considerable sum in silver; but seeing the Prelate return to the charge, *he went in where the plate was; he took vessels of gold and of silver, broke them up and then gave them to St. Germain*. When Louis the Fat died, *he spread*, say elsewhere these same Chronicles, *all his treasure among churches and the poor, and all his plate of gold and of silver*. St. Louis himself had a similar one; and below will be found several pieces cited in Charles V's inventory, which had come, as an inheritance, into the hands of this last Monarch.

Again, the luxury in question was, for many centuries, almost the only means which Kings, Princes and Great-Lords had to display their riches and their magnificence. Thus some could push it to a point hard to believe. In the following Chapter will be read the description of a famous banquet given in 1457, at Tours, by the Count de Foix, when the Ambassadors of Ladislas of Austria came to ask Charles VI for his daughter Madelaine to marry their master. Then, at this meal, there were twelve tables of seven services each; and, for each service, there were, at each table one hundred forty silver plates. Let one, from this item alone, calculate what an immense quantity of plate the Count must have possessed. It stuns the imagination. Today, despite these enormous masses of gold and silver which America has sent us for three centuries, the most powerful Sovereign of Europe could barely offer such magnificence. And after that people come, I will keep repeating it, to praise to us the simplicity of former times.

List of the plate of Charles V

But, so that my readers can see in detail how far this kind of magnificence went with Sovereigns, I am going to give the inventory of what Charles V owned, this Prince nicknamed the Wise, and who deserved to be so called. He himself ordered it inventoried in 1379; and the original of this inventory still survives in the King's Library. I was not able to consult it, because, for two years, the part of the Library in which are these manuscripts is forbidden to the public for the indispensable repairs it required. But the Abbé de Choisy has given the extract of it in the life he published of the Monarch; and it is after the Abbé's notice that the list you are about to read was prepared.

General inventory of Charles the Fifth of all the treasures he had of gold as of silver. That is, crowns, helmets, plate, church ornaments, and other things encrusted with stones; and also jewels, fully worked plate of gold and silver, being from Chateaus, Hotels and Oratories of the said Lord, in his Chateaus of Meleun-sur-Seyne [Melun-sur-Seine]*; from the Vincennes woods, from the Louvre, from St. Germain-en-Laye, from his Hotels of St. Pol in Paris, of Beauté-sur-Marne, and elsewhere; and also ornaments and plate which are continually carried with him; and with that of all the Chapels, chambers of embroidery and tapestry of the said Lord; which inventory was begun to be made by the said Lord the XXIth day of January in the year MCCCCLXXIX, etc.*

> No[te]. I omit here everything to do with crowns, reliquaries, church ornaments, rings, and jewels, etc.

Silver Plate.

Four dozen very large platters.

Twelve dozen small ones.

Twenty dozen bowls (sort of plates).

Five shaving bowls.

And what is more an infinity of *justes*, hyders, quarts, pots, pints, ewers, *coquemars*, alms bowls (a), hanaps, cups, comfet-boxes, basins, vessels, etc.

Gilded Silver Plate

Twenty nefs.

The great nef of King Jean, having at each end a castle, and, all about, towers, weighing..... 70 marks.

> (a) So were called a piece of plate in which the Sovereign's Officers threw, during his meal, some pieces of meat to give the poor.

Twenty-five flagons.

Two other flagons representing in relief the nine Worthies... 197

Fifty basins.

A basin bearing the arms of France.... 35

A shaving bowl with fleurs-de-lis sculpted on the rim... 14

Four dozen large platters.

Six dozen small.

Four large tarred and enameled platters, each weighing....10

Two old fruit plates, having each on their edges three closed fleurs-de-lis in the style of arms...... .9 m. 6 ounces

Nineteen dozen bowls.

Six dozen candle-holders.

Twenty salt cellars..

A large salt cellar, bearing the arms of France, and given by the Bishop of Noyon....... 28

Eighteen spoons.

And further an infinity of barrels, *estamoyes*, *justes*, pots, pints, ewers, alms pots, cups, hanaps, bowls, goblets, comfet-boxes, etc.

GOLDEN PLATE

A large nef, borne by six lions, enameled with France, and bearing at each end an Angel......	53 marks	4 onc.
Another nef, borne by four lions...	29	1
Large nef given by the city of Paris......	125	

Small nef, having at each end a serpent.....	31	
A bucket, held by four sirens.......	25	1
Twenty-five basins.		
Two basins for washing the hands, strewn with miniature arms of France on the edges...	19	
Twelve candle-holders.		
Two other candle-holders bearing the arms of France, and given by M. de Chevreuse as a holiday gift.	18	2
Two flagons, with two buffalo from which the handle hangs...	47	7
Six enameled *estamoyes*, each with cover.....	177	
Six large *justes with a round enamel of France*.......	118	
Twelve other round *justes* bearing the arms of France.....	117	6
Two hyders, bearing on each side a savage armed with a spear, bearing, in front, the head of a lion; behind, an enamel with images; and on the base, six enamels of France......	41	1
A quart strewn with enamels of the arms of France and of England	6	6
A square pot, strewn with enamels of France........	7	4
A large alms pot, bearing four arms of France, and two lions as a handle...	36	5
Cup of St. Louis with its ewer.......	7	6
Cup of King Dagobert.....	4	

Two hanaps.

Forty cups.

Nineteen goblets.

Twelve unmatched ewers.

Eight comfet-boxes.

Thirty-six large platters, all the same........	227	4
Twelve other large platters, of another design......	72	
Thirty-six others for fruit, stamped on the sides.....	56	1
Six dozen bowls....	217	5
A large salt cellar in the shape of a nef, given by the city of Paris...	15	6

Ten other salt cellars.

Thirty spoons.

Golden plate encrusted with stones

Cup of Charlemagne enriched with sapphires........	5 marks	5 onc
Hanap on a tripod, garnished with pearls, rubies and emeralds.... .	6	6

Thirty seven goblets.

Forty ewers.

Forty flagons.

Forty-two pots, pints and *chopines*.

Forty-five salt cellars.

Forty-five comfet-boxes.

Forty-three spoons, and forks.

I say nothing of the considerable weight, of the form and the bizarre ornaments of several of these pieces; such was the taste of the time. But these ornaments themselves, the sculpting, the figures in relief, the enamels they bore, prove that Paris then had both famous Silversmiths, and Artists in more than one genre.

Enamels

It is claimed that the art of painting in enamel on metal only began in France towards 1632. That is an error; since several pieces of Charles V's plate were enameled. Palissy himself (1580) informs us that, in his time, the Enamellers of Limoges for three sous gave a dozen of those images of signs which were then worn in the hat; *which signs were so well worked, and their enamels so good, fused evenly on the copper, that there was no painting as agreeable* (a).

Custom of putting arms or marks on silver

It must have been noticed, further, that in the plate of Charles V, there were only a few pieces which bore his coat of arms; the rest were not marked with arms; which is all the more remarkable in that, in all elegant affairs, the Nobility then showed off its arms. Not only did they bedeck all the persons attached to their service with them; but they themselves wore them all over their clothes. I have said above, in the article on desserts, that in meals it was a gallantry of the time to give the person one wanted to feast their arms in sugar paste, or otherwise.

(a) The reputation of the Enamellers of Limoges still survived at the end of the last century. The Memoir which the Intendant of this Province provided in 1692, by order of the King, to the Duke of Burgundy on the state of the Generality, mentions them. *Their works would have beauty*, he says, *if the Workers had more knowledge and taste for Drawing and Painting.*

In the first times of the Monarchy, the custom was to put the initials of one's name, or even one's whole name, on the different pieces of silver one possessed. Proofs of this are seen in the will of St. Remy Among the things he leaves, he counts *cochlearia tria qua suo sunt nomine titulata* [three spoons bearing his name].

[Closing thoughts]

What will not be less surprising is this immense quantity of pots, flagons, ewers, and other such decorative vessels offered by Charles V's inventory. All that served to decorate the King's treasure, on the days when he allowed it to be shown to the public; or to adorn his three dressers in official banquets. Further, there were occasions where this plate could be used. Such was the meal which the Monarch gave in the Palace to the Emperor his uncle. His tables being of more than eight hundred settings, one sees very well that nothing was too much for the service of such a multitude. Also he had a large part of his plate carried with him everywhere he went. The inventory says it specifically.

On the other hand, when one recalls that all these riches had been amassed by a Prince who had inherited a ruined Kingdom, which had had to maintain against England very expensive and very long wars, which finally only enjoyed a very limited revenue, one cannot contain one's surprise. Louis XIV, himself, Louis XIV, the most magnificent of our Princes, did not display, in the days of his glory, such magnificence. When in 1709, he had his plate taken to the Mint, that of silver only produced 1,400,000 livres; and that of gold, 400,000. It is Mme. de Maintenon who informs us of this fact in her letters. Now, how could King Charles V have procured such a treasure! Or rather, how did the Nation, in a time when the mines of America did not yet exist for the Europeans, draw to itself enough metal that the wisest of its Kings used, without inconvenience and without complaints, so great a quantity in such useless luxury? The response to the second of these questions would provide matter for a very interesting dissertation; but it is not within my subject.

As for the first, I have already satisfied it in advance. This so numerous plate was not the fruit of Charles' economies. Certain pieces, as I have said, and as the inventory proves, came to him, by inheritance, from the Kings his predecessors. Others had been given to him; the inventory proves it as well. It is very likely even that these gift pieces formed, although the List says nothing of this, a large part of his plate; since then the custom was that the Great, the Municipalities; even individuals, sometimes make such offerings. Finally, a certain quantity was the fruit of his victories. I have presented above a passage from Monstrelet which demonstrates it. Probably, during the Monarch's wars, other cities bought, at the same price as Metz, freedom from pillage or ransoming.

With time, the attitudes and customs of which we have just read the history, changed. As Royal power gathered solidity and strength, it stopped making its grandeur known in numerous plate which it displayed in spectacle on certain days. It built magnificent palaces, which all the arts as desired rushed to beautify. There, as in the center of its glory, it has known to concentrate all the Greats, who composed for it a Court as brilliant as it was submissive. Instead of these nefs, these flagons, and these golden platters which it once used to represent it, it surrounded itself with a numerous military and civil Household, which, unfortunately onerous for the State by the excessive multiplication of its members, nonetheless offers to its subjects as to foreigners the united spectacle of magnificence and of strength, of power and of majesty.

www.ingramcontent.com/pod-product-compliance
Lightning Source LLC
Chambersburg PA
CBHW070204290526

45789CB00002B/913